The Wizard and The Wrench

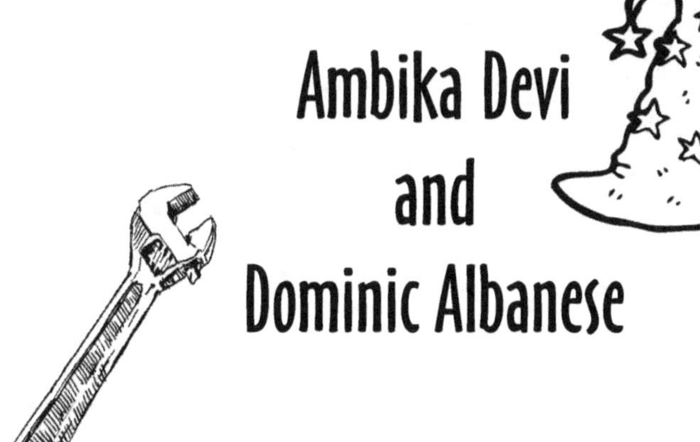

Ambika Devi
and
Dominic Albanese

The Wizard and The Wrench

Ambika Devi

and

Dominic Albanese

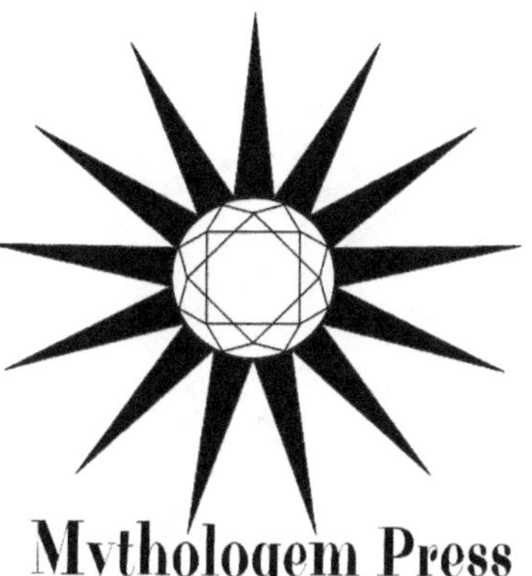

Mythologem Press

Publishing Literary Brilliance

The Wizard and the Wrench

The Wizard and The Wrench

Library of Congress Catalog-in-Publication Data
Ford, Amy a.k.a. Ambika Devi, MA 1959-
Albanese, Dominic 1945-
ISBN-13: 978-0-9978678-2-4
ISBN-10: 0-9978678-2-5

For information contact:
Mythologem Press
www.MythologemPress.com
VOX 772-233-8229
MythologemPress@gmail.com
www.TheWizardandTheWrench.com

FIRST EDITION

Designed by Ambika Devi, Ron Birchenough and Catalina Rueda
Cover art by Ambika Devi and Matt Sturgess of 4th Avenue Photography
Artwork by Ambika Devi and Spain Rodriguez
Photography by Ambika Devi, Catalina Rueda, Cristine Bezembinder Wyant of Play Date Photography, Summer Moon, Rusti Lee, Gary Peckham, Michael Orchard, and Matt Sturgess
Manuscript completed June 20, 2017, 02:20:22 p.m.

Printed in the United States of America

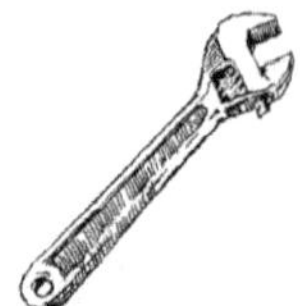

Table of Contents

The Wizard and the Wrench

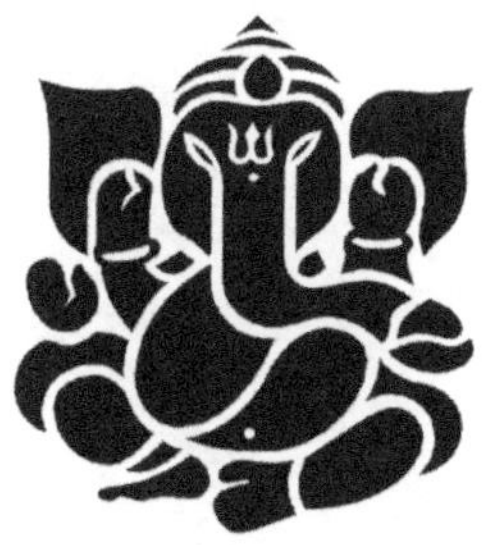

With many blessings of Ganesha!

Introduction

Get ready to carve out some quality time for words this season.

In *The Wizard and The Wrench*, a collaborative work of poetry by Ambika Devi and Dominic Albanese, the congruent paradox of ascending imagery provokes great wordplay as you page through multilayered sections, providing rife lingua franca—a fine fodder for the imagination.

"Each bead leads to the next/shimmering ..." plucking a sprig of sound salad, they complete a sublime ritual of vast textual fascinations—something like an exquisite paisley woven rug with lemons and limes scattered about delightedly, together providing "counterpoint rhythm/ and rhyme/shaking my soul/to awaken."

Cutting the syllabic molecules through and through with a wizened clarity, with the air of twisting prose delicately and sublimely melded into metaphysically regulating, exquisite sound, these two writers perpetuate positive and syncopated ear candy, simultaneously packed with language nutrition—*aixo era y no era* (it was and it was not)—and provide us with a singularly exotic pleasure. It is a wordsicle fit for the finest gourmands of linguistic delicacies.

I hope you enjoy these treasured sounds as much as I did, as both a feast for the soul as well as a massage for the ears, mind, and chakras.

With Sincerity,
Dr. Patagonia, poet

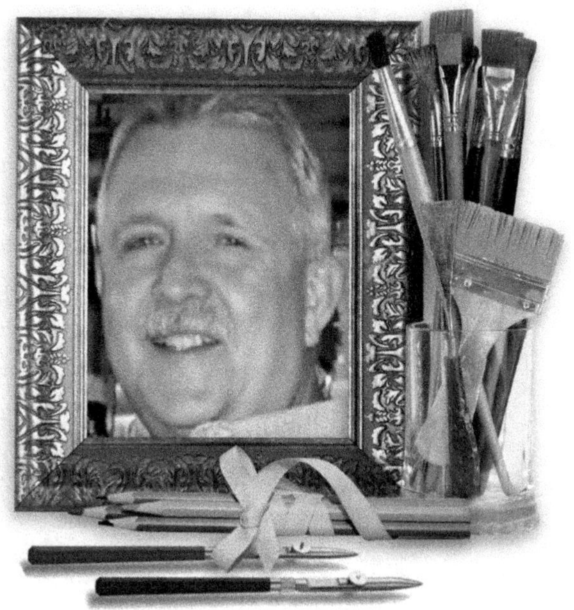

We dedicate this book to our dear friend **Ron Birchenough** who flew off from the encumbrance of a physical body and guided us from the other side to get this project done. Our hearts are dripping with the sweet honey of compassion for all who miss this creative spirit. Ron gave so much love and creativity to this project and for this we are eternally grateful.

With love, The Wizard and The Wrench

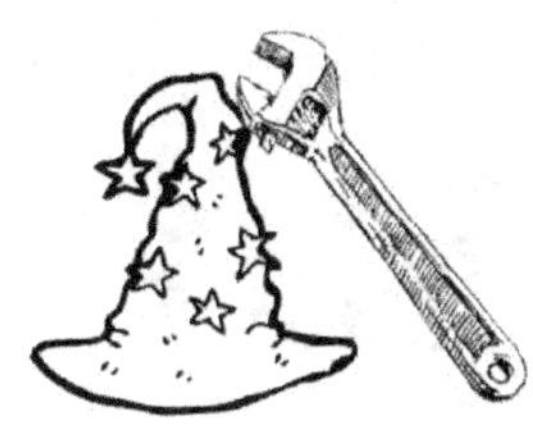

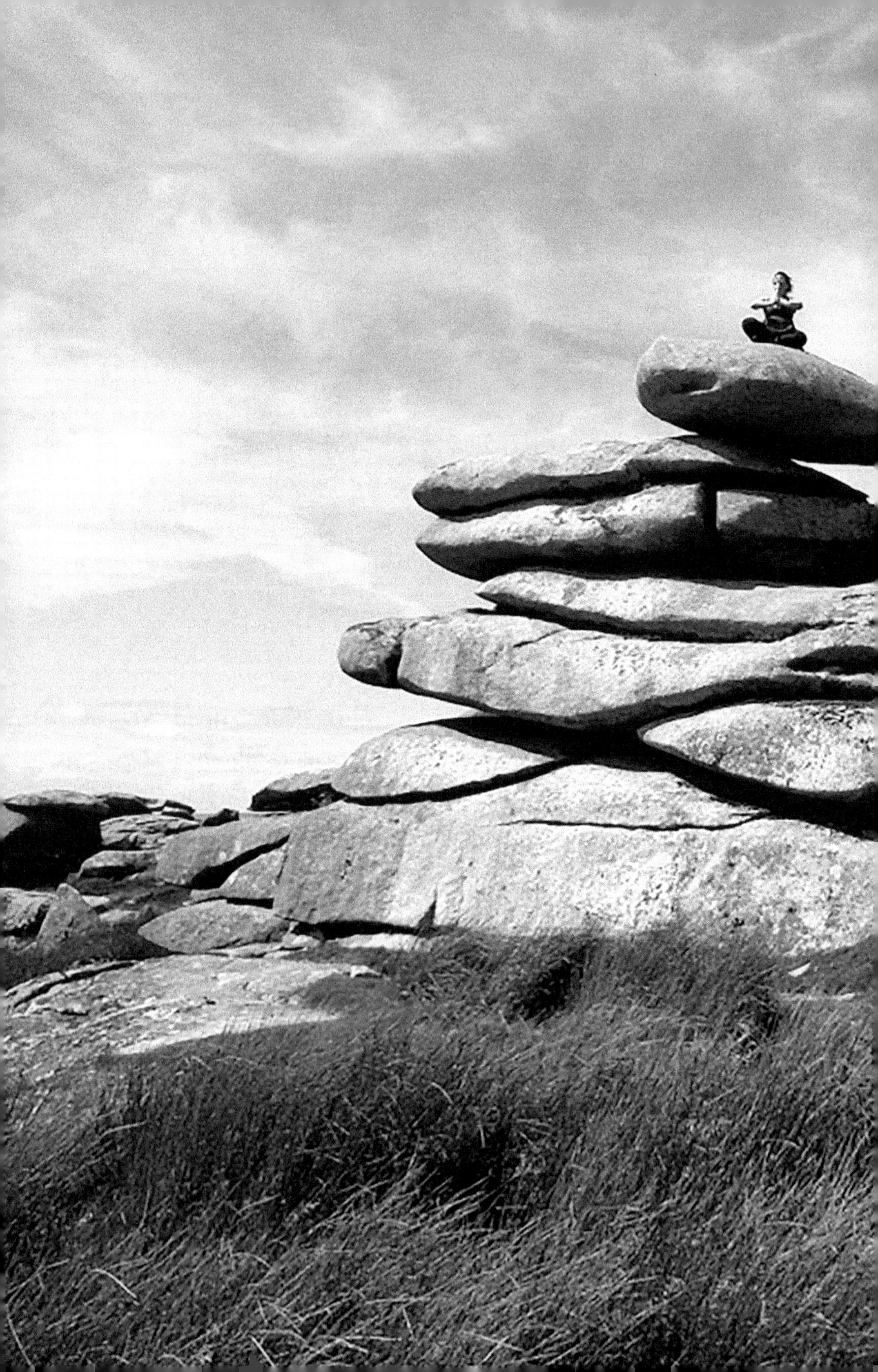

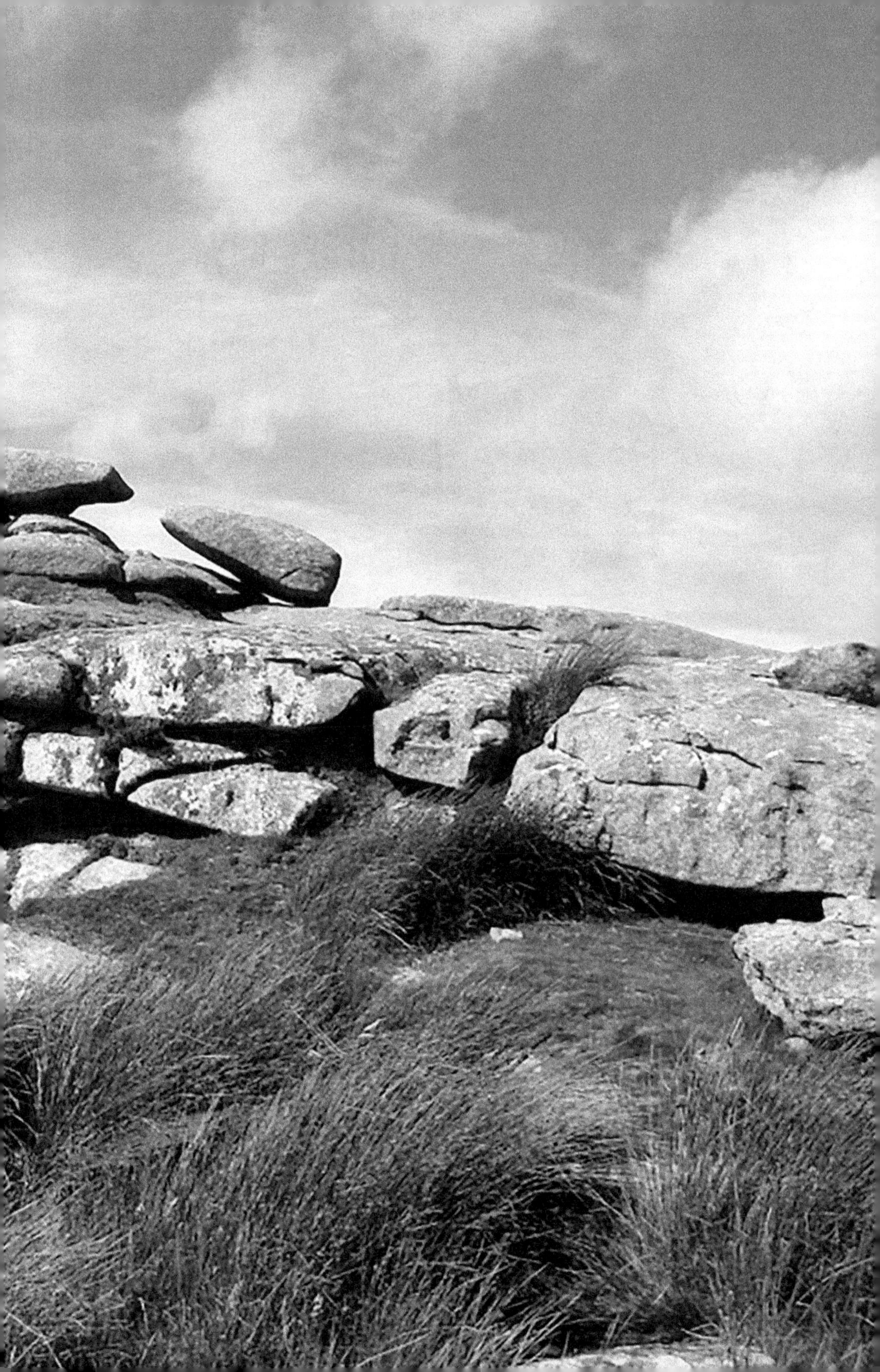

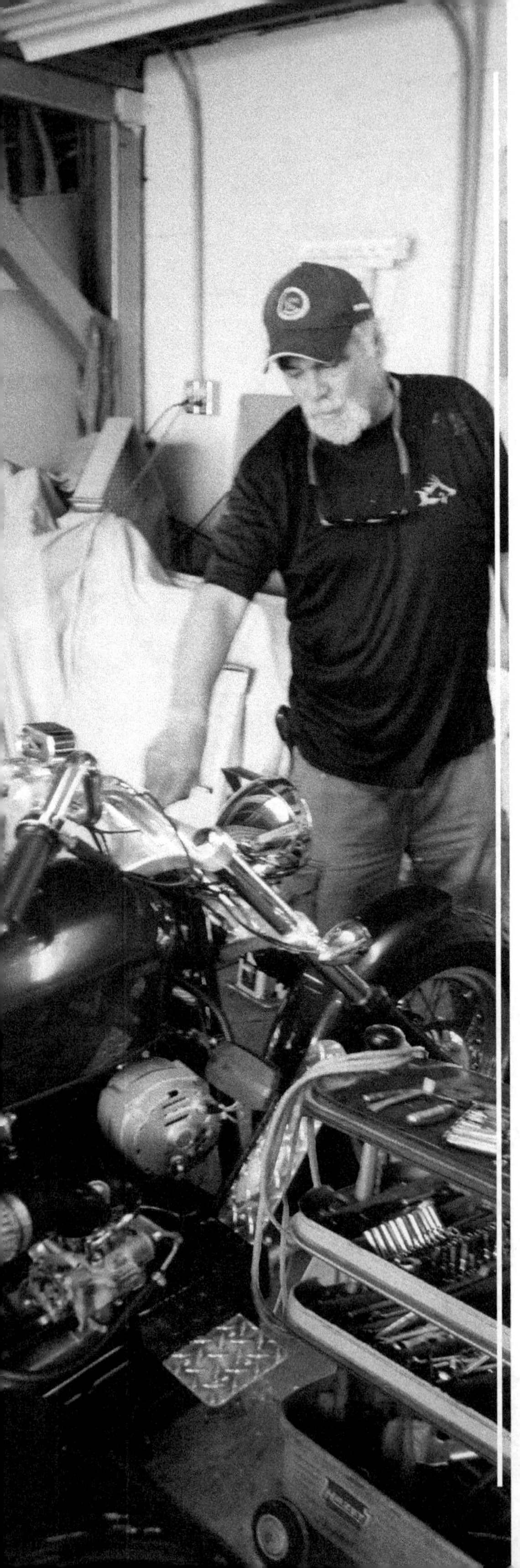

Garage day

motor oil

gear lube

are

part

of

my DNA

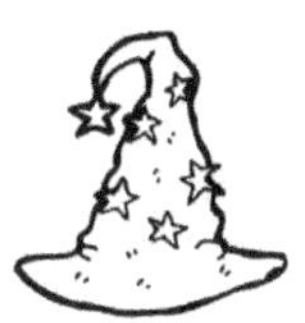

Beads the shaman strung for me

Maybe they are not shiny like pearls
but they are filled with love and wisdom
many hours of deep contemplation
facing fears and demons
purging in the garden
releasing perceptions
of past hurt and mistakes
learning to love life and spirit
once again
in celebratory healing

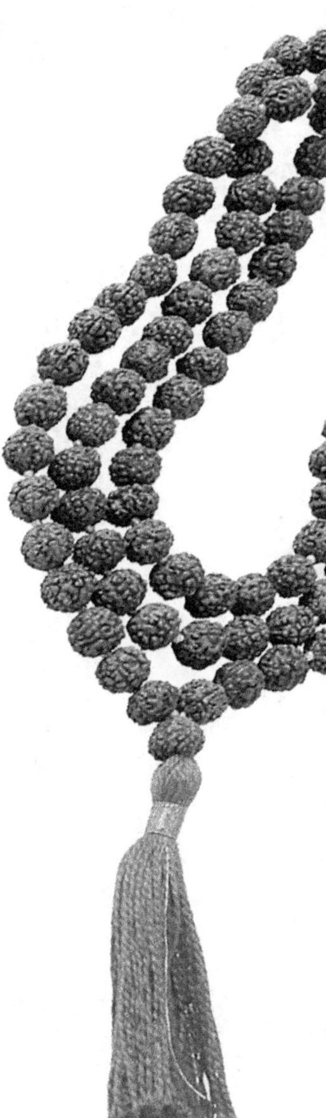

Each bead leads to the next
shimmering
catching light
marking the steps of the journey
encircling the physical boundaries
a gateway to the
psyche

Every lesson
slipping through the eye of the needle
then the eye of the next bead

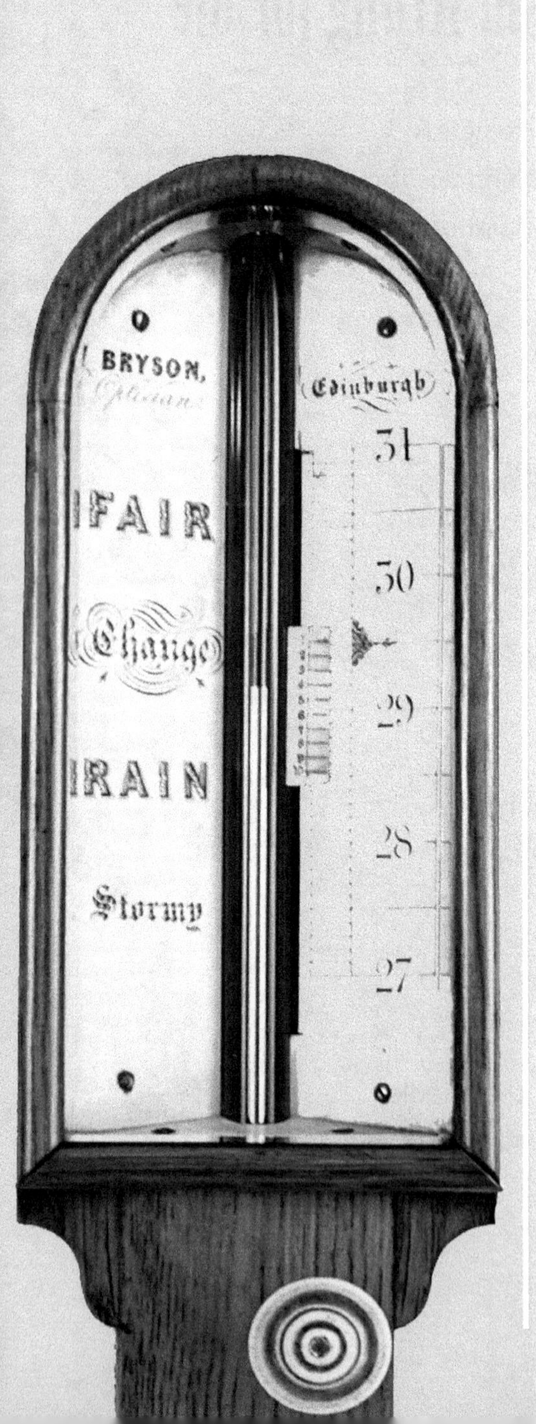

Barometric

atmospheric
alterations
in pressure
temperature
premature
ancient
enhancement
allow
all manner
of life
to flourish
or flounder
about
much like
thinking
about
you
does me

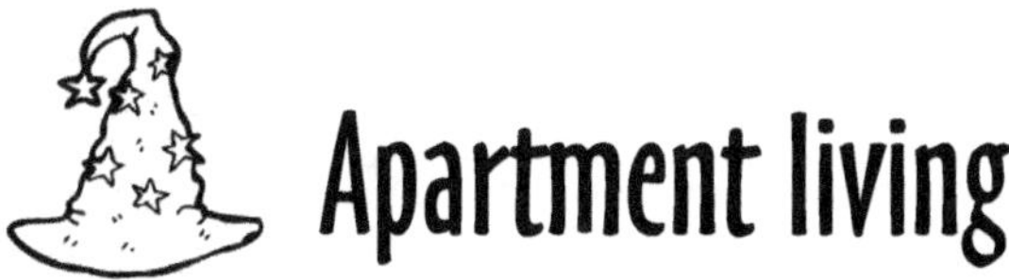

Apartment living

The building burned down
orange glow
on my window
I saw you smoking
curly hair
small dog
a lady
from the far side
you are freaking me out
thinking this is damn good cheese
wanting you
on my cracker
spreading out for me
neighbors having sex
transformative energy
wishing it was me
it is way more fun with a friend
do you know one I could call?

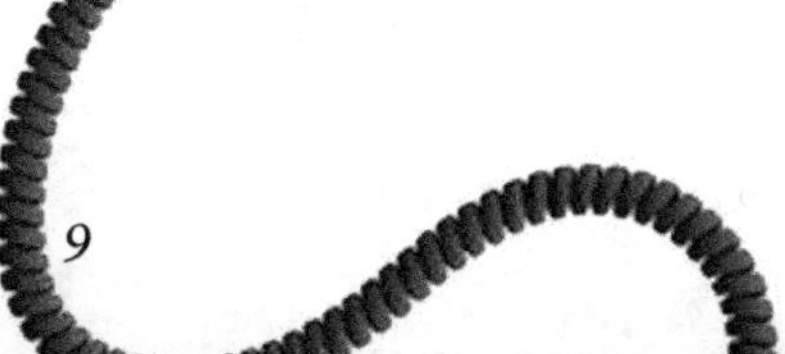

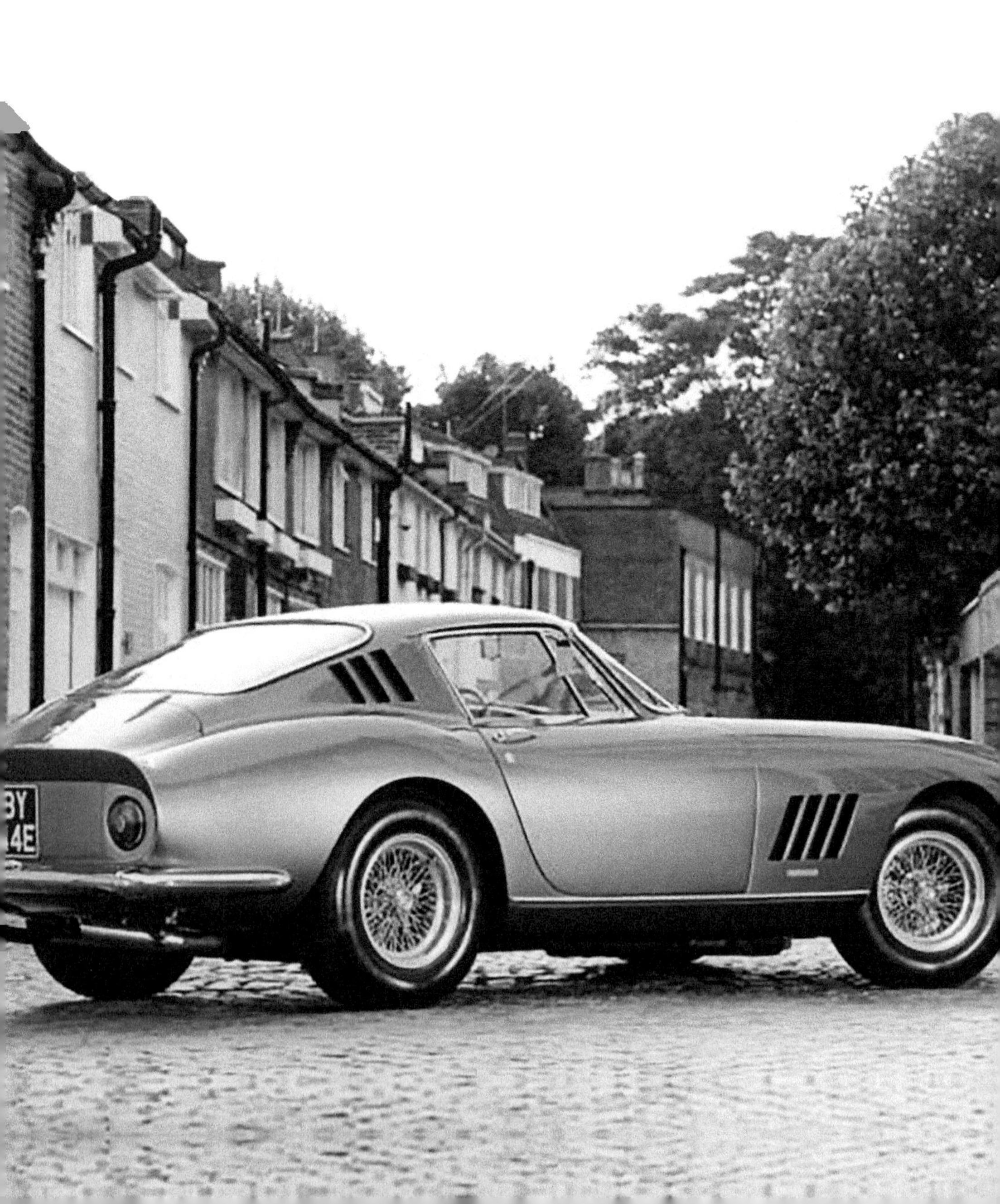

Never forget

You and I are not allowed
"Class envy"
Couple blue collar boys
who hit the
big time
Yeah yeah I know you in F40s or 355s
But
How a Coney Island kid
got his hands on a
N.A.R.T. Daytona...drove to Petaluma
Cross the G.C. Bridge
in triple digits
Or
first run 308s glass body
N 4 webbers...with Borani pipes

Or some other exotic
iron we got
to fold fondle 'n smoke tires in

Nope
Brain pan HD video cam
of that turn on 205 headed to Camas
in the wind song engine at symphony sound
the days of fine old Italian cars
we could not afford
the tires for

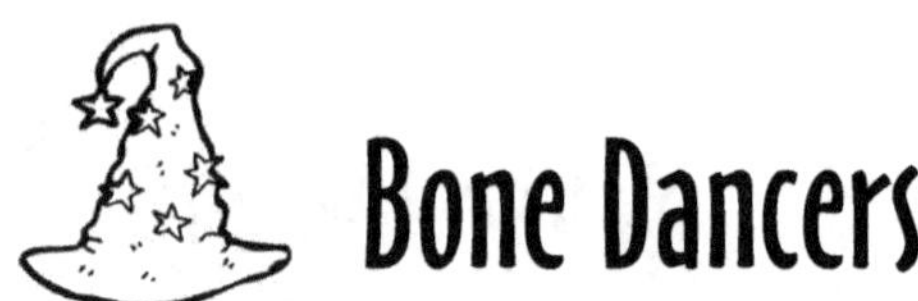

Bone Dancers

I remember
when I lived
with the Bone Dancers
the ones who reveled
in the release
don't get me wrong
I truly appreciate this precious gift
and do my best
to move through the day
to sing and bless each living thing
come
let us spiral
and serve
at Mother's
slithery
feet

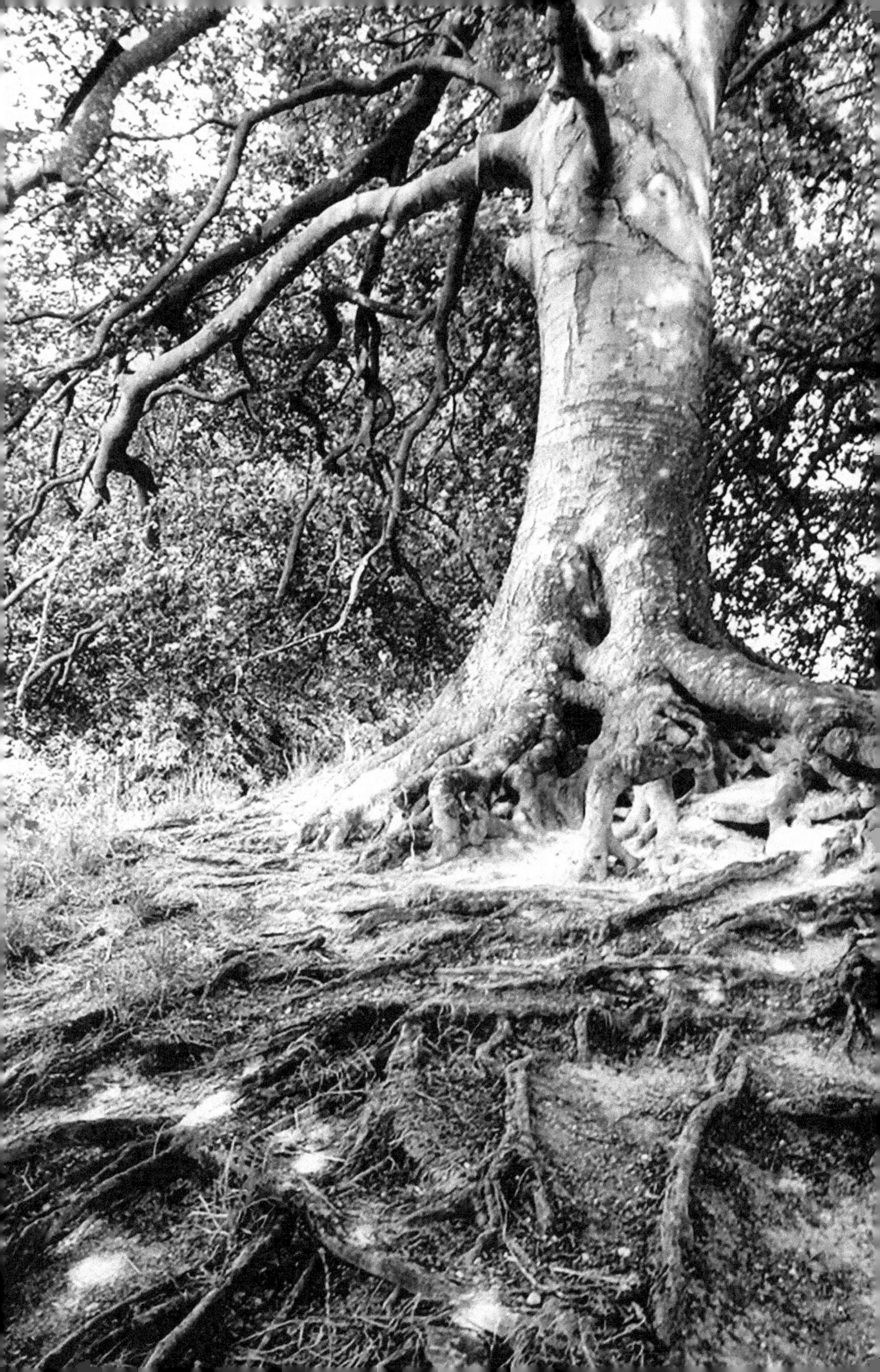

Seasonal affective disorder

Up Oregon way
it was the rain
the lack of light

Down heah
it be a whole different
set of reactions
yup
by 8:22 am
be hot enough
hot enough
with a small
wind
ya can still
mow, move, set

But by 11:00
ya betta be
in da ice tea
and da A/C
affective disorder
rules

There are
ways around
the heat
beach, boat, pool
yet
can't complain
it's all part
of the big game

tell ya what though
that buzz ya hear
when the fan kicks on
that
is
the sound
of salvation

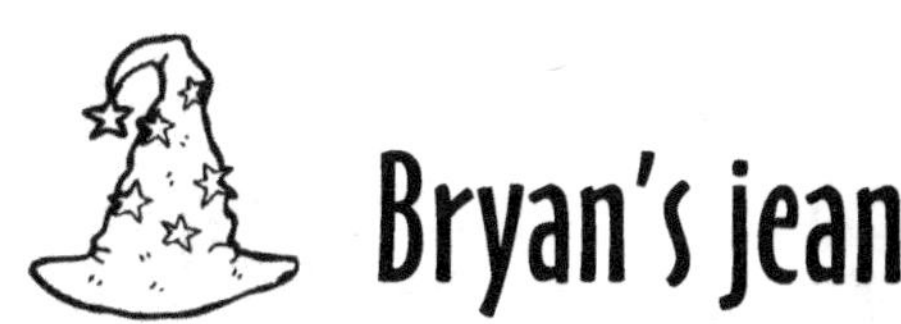

Bryan's jeans

You know
those are Bryan's jeans
she said with a smile
Isn't it amazing?
I guess she just can't believe
that we've occupied the same spaces so intimately
I can feel where his knees were
and imagine how those holes got there
in the crotch and butt
she says "those jeans came from the Gap you know"
and everyone hummed with interest

She's followed me in there may times
but I never buy anything
I just touch

Those jeans fit you great people tell me
and I smile and say
thanks
thinking

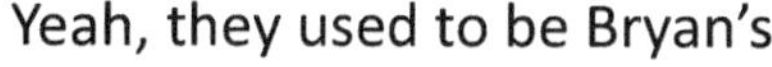

Yeah, they used to be Bryan's

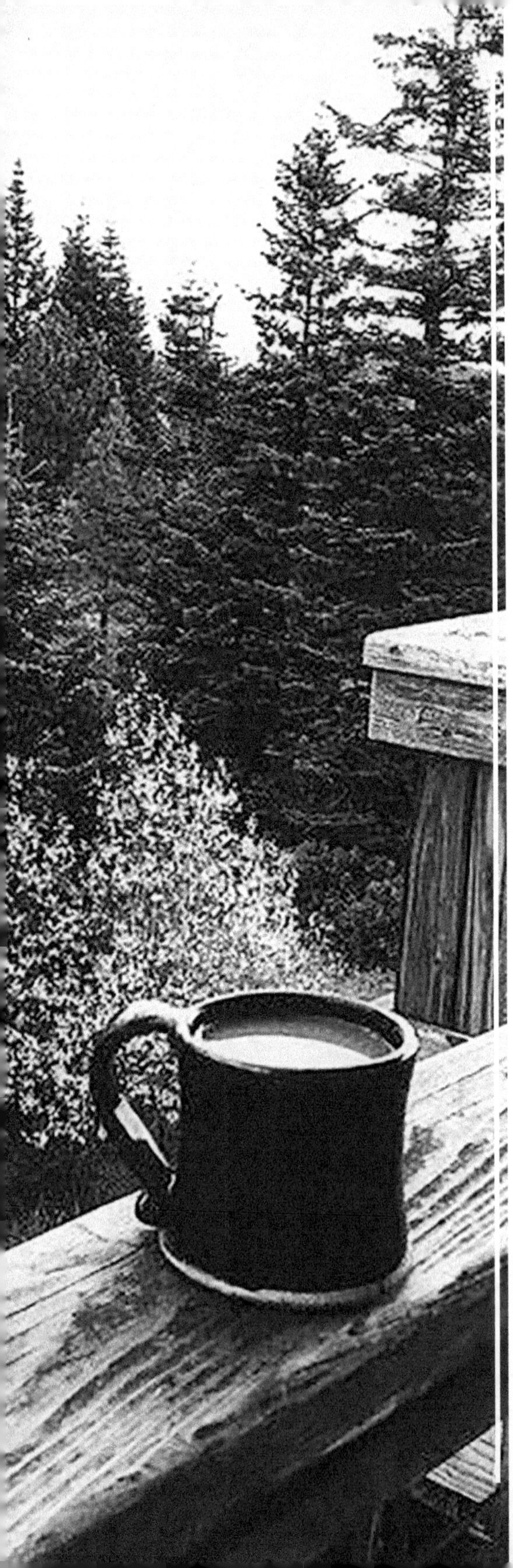

Between

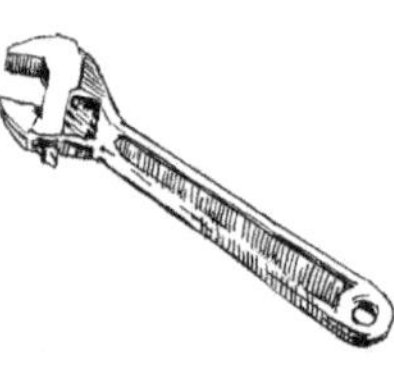

old love songs

a

cup of my very

special coffee

‘n

three bright colored birds

on

the fence

there

is

no place else

no

more

words

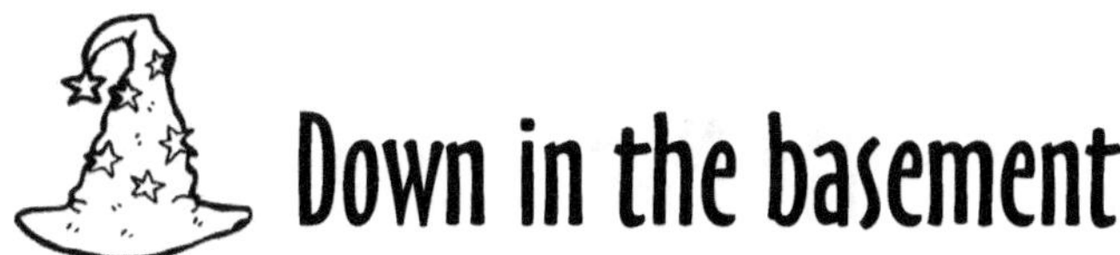

Down in the basement

Down in the basement
the sound of steam
coming from an iron
and a foreign tongue
under the breath of a tiny woman

Ritual starching of unwanted creases in my Levis
was her magic
My granny was a mystic

Small pieces of paper
with symbols and glyphs
that looked like archeological finds
were brought out by candlelight
when it was just the two of us

So tight was her grip on me
that I knew this was the most important event
I would ever witness

Healing laughter
that wrapped around and warmed me
like the afghans she crocheted

My Nana

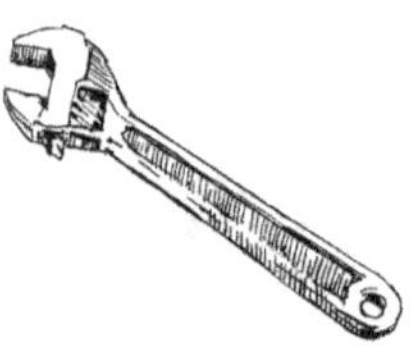

My nana
would always say
sin salta sin sabor

no salt no flavor

over the ole wood
stove in
Vermont
when I was a little boy

she would cook
for us
sing to us
give us lasagna
love
to keep us
safe from darkness

all the years
of my bitter tears
the smell of
that kitchen
has kept with me

even if she went
away forever
so
long
ago

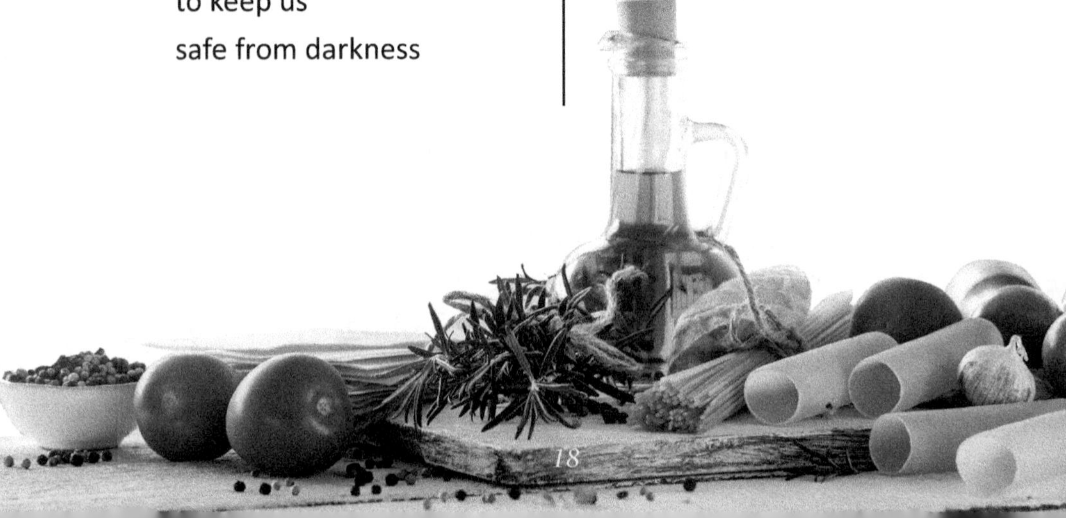

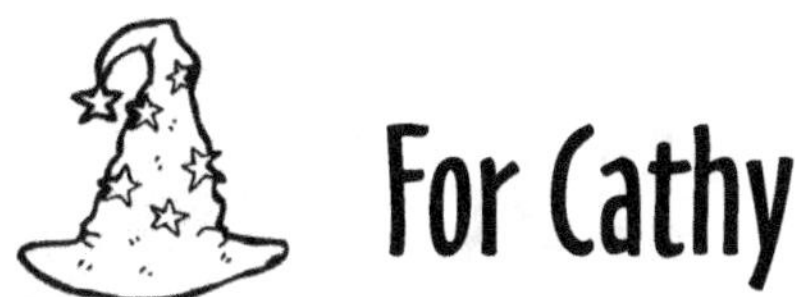

For Cathy

She says "You're gonna have to listen to me rant because I'm in one of those 'Everything is so right and I'm feeling so blue' moods, maybe it's PMS or that every time I get comfortable I need to change something."

I say, "Good things happen when blue is a part of it, like once in a Blue Moon is when those wishes finally come true. Jeans are blue and everyone is always scrambling to get into them or out of them on the weekends, and look at Picasso, I really dug his blue period! The ocean is blue, at least from certain viewpoints, and you know we are oceans apart from the rest of humanity."

She says "Honestly, I'm so weary of people. I feel like I'm a ghost wandering among them, observing and puzzling at their behavior and choices. What IS it they're trying to say? How DO they perceive themselves? Do they REALLY take themselves SERIOUSLY?"

"Yeah, I'm afraid so" I say, "Serious as spending time in the fray, letting them drain us, walking around like vampires, white faces reflecting the sunlight and sooty lips saying nothing I want to hear."

I ask her "When are you going to give in to the fact that we are the ones who caught the golden beam of light on our way in? I'm not saying that we're higher or better, just that we're receiving on satellite dish and they just got their first pair of rabbit ears at Radio Shack."

So I think for a minute and add "Perhaps chocolate is the Messiah and maybe we should just devote ourselves to it."

There

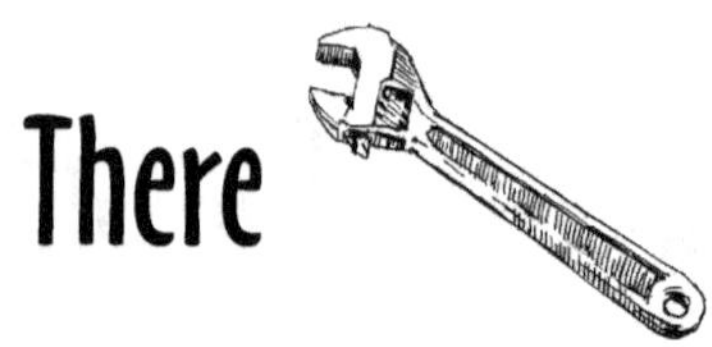

There is still a lot
pass time
now dated time of alternate reality
either with words
or with lovers
roundabout way
or memory wall
lurking today in my brain pan
Nancy 'n' I ate a handful of 'shrooms
were linked in right brain, left brain
fibro-cellular chemical psychedelic aware + oblivious
yet ... we both sat on a San Francisco hillside
positive if we tried to walk
we would fly off and be swallowed bay water
dunked ... laughing ... gazing at each other
kaleidoscope bug eyes ... dreaming wide awake as we
wandered her house
at day's end ... she stared at her wall
told
me she always knew she picked correct colors
painted ... but was now sure of it
for that afternoon we were one person in two bodies
then came real life again

She went off to China …
I fell into a cocaine ditch
fell deeper …
to points of near terminal velocity
On her return …
ultimate sadness,
"What have you done?"
there were no words to answer
she left …
went to Bali,
never came back or sent a postcard
life … now … is looking back
on thirty-eight years ago
with not a shred of guilt
sandstorm dust bunny bad mojo
or
who I was I am not now
every few years
I look at her picture …
there is no reason to cry
That one afternoon
we were one person in two bodies …
if ya get that gold ring once
rejoice and be glad in it
now
alone … surrounded with books
shadow bones bits of paper
argue with my own what if's
or whatever's in … time

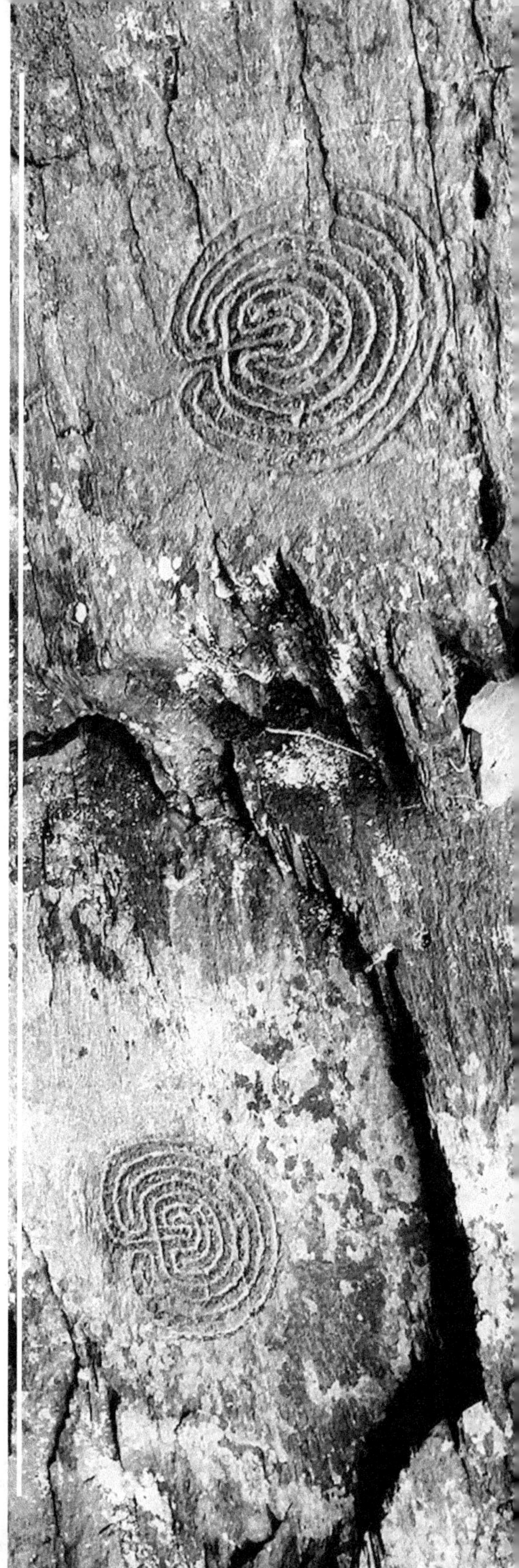

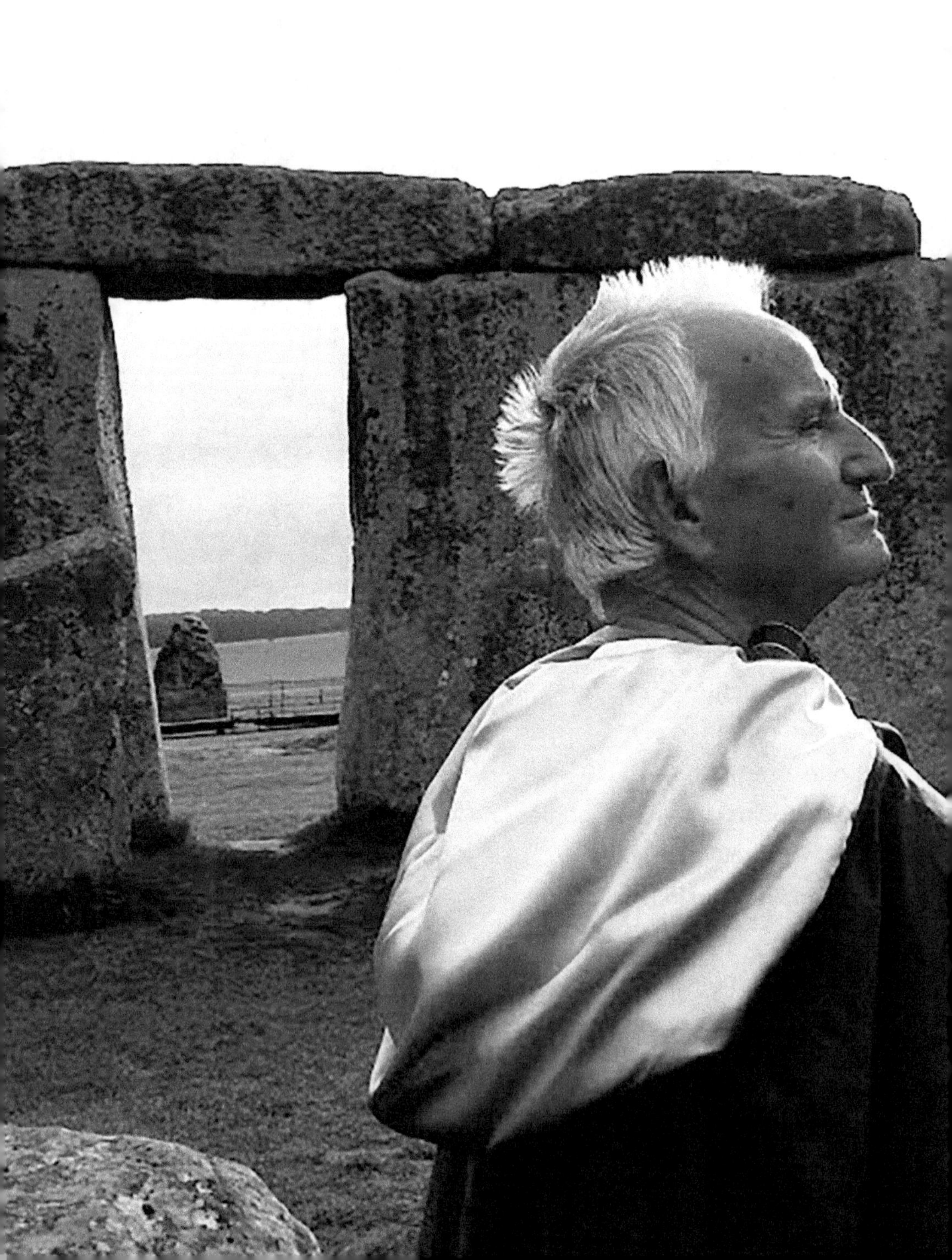

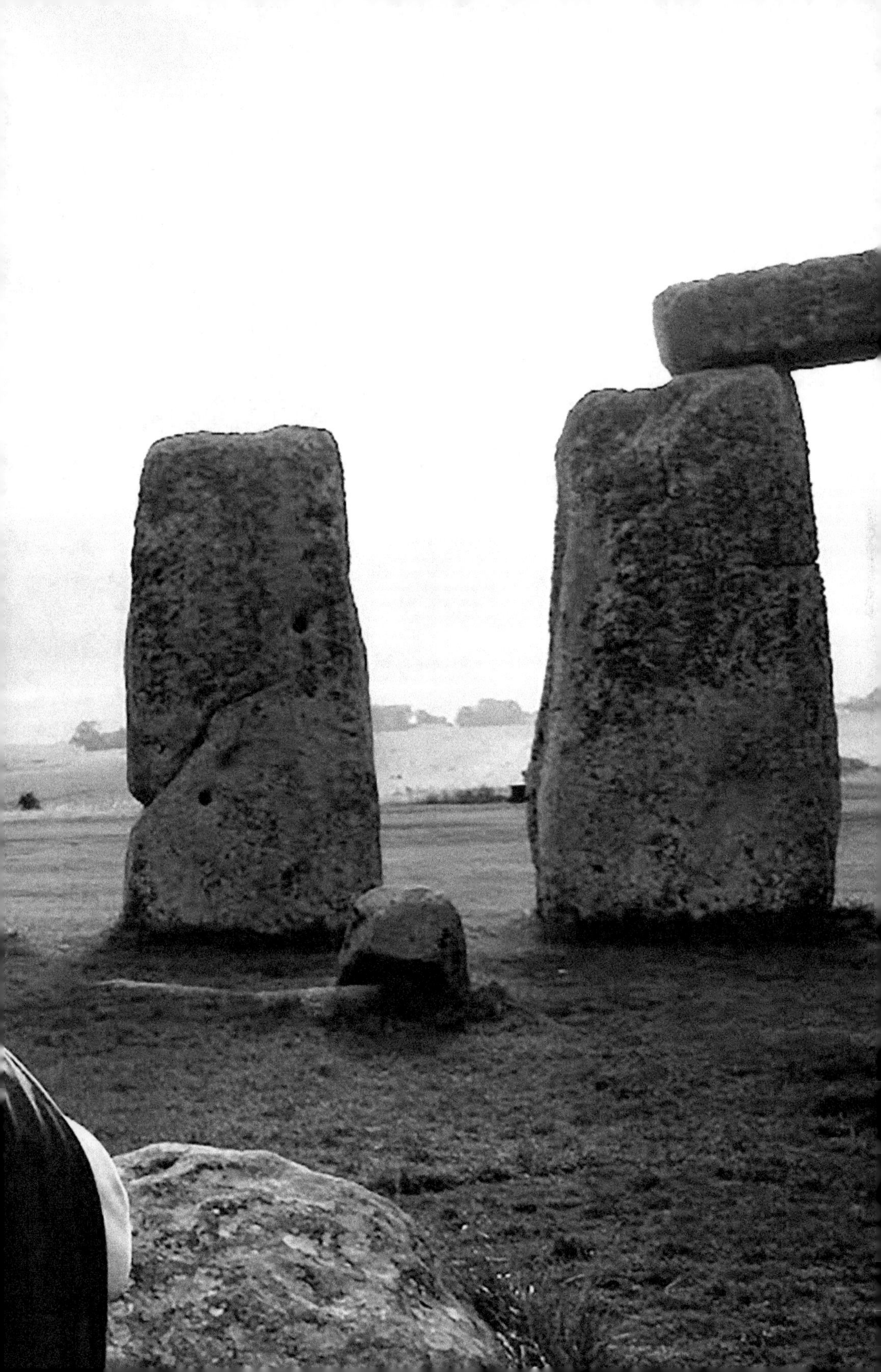

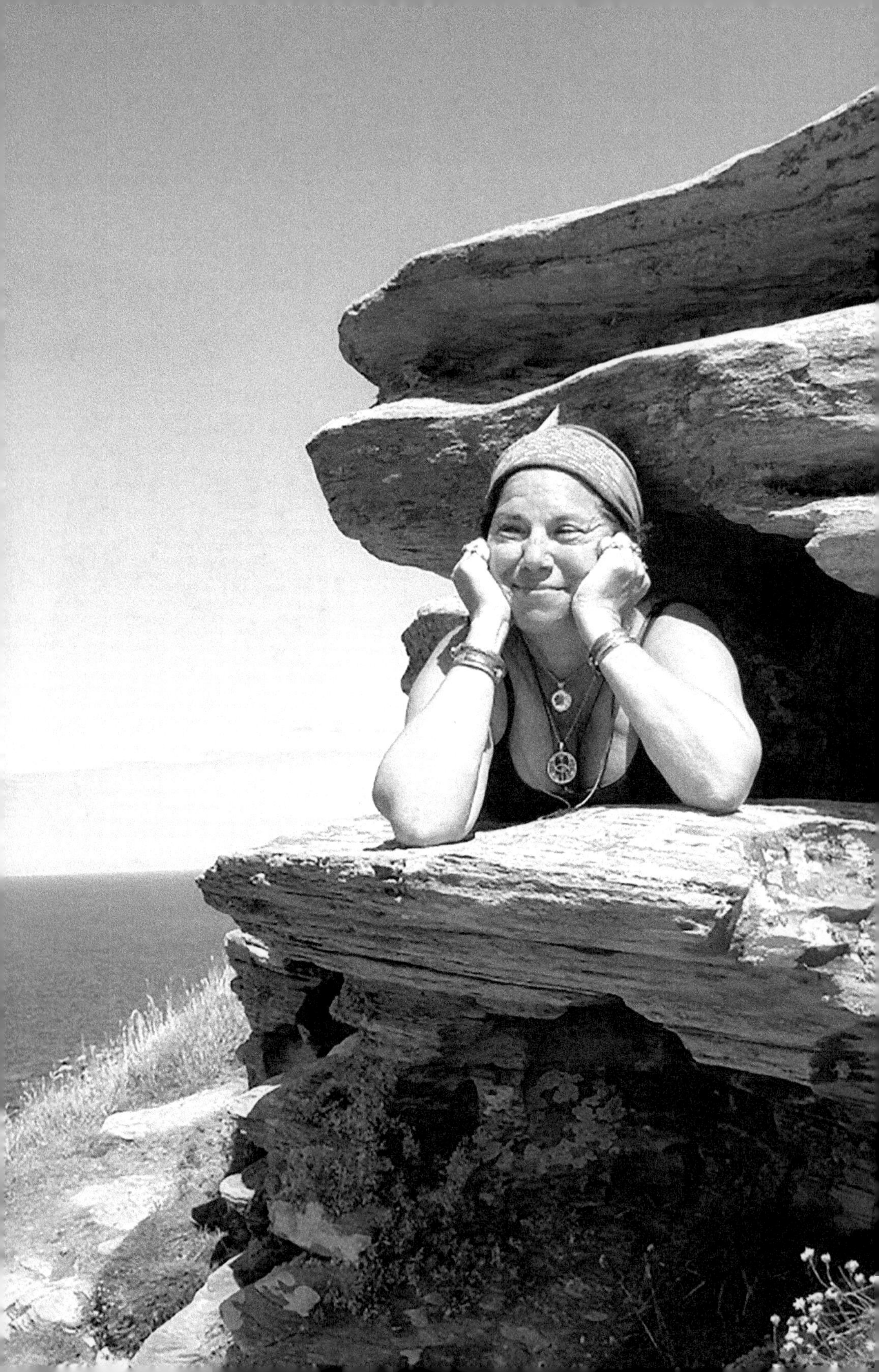

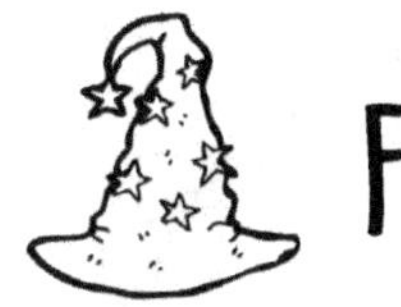

From the future

a strange blip
a beep
you ring from a different hemisphere
smiling and calling me *hermanita,* little sister
of course I miss you
small square of liquid you
is never enough

stumbling upon
opportunity
perhaps
destiny
revealing the future
leaving this place
retreating to mountains

in hopes
of making a change
for generations to come

The reason

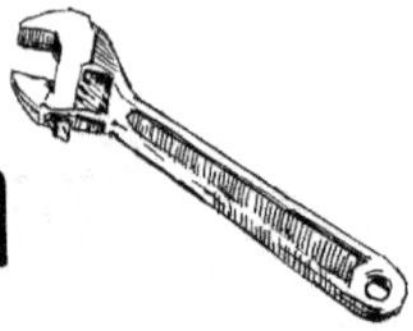

The days
of wanting to be
anyone but me
are gone now
my brother's ghost
is right over
the next ridge
waiting
for me
to
tell
more
truth

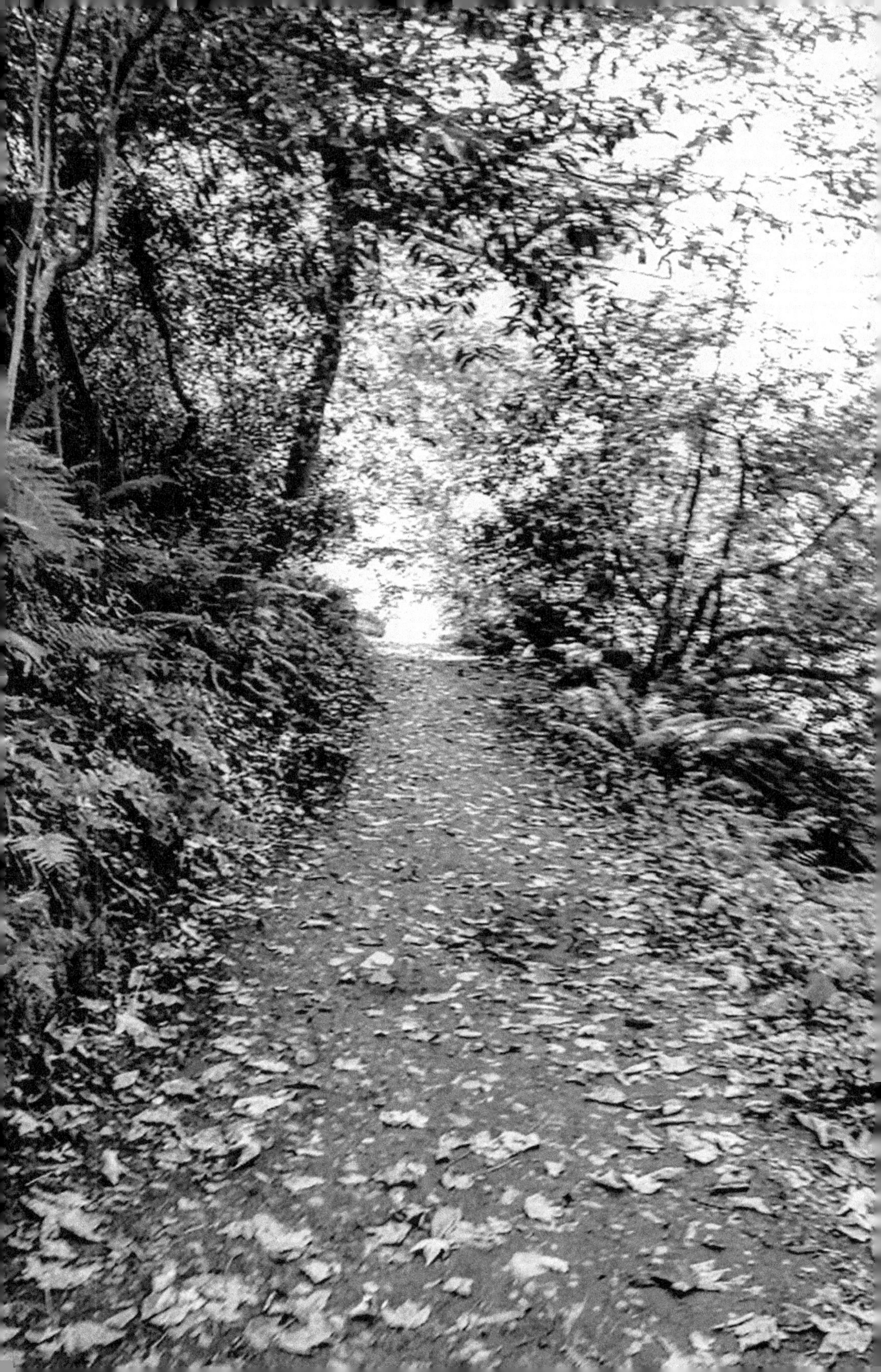

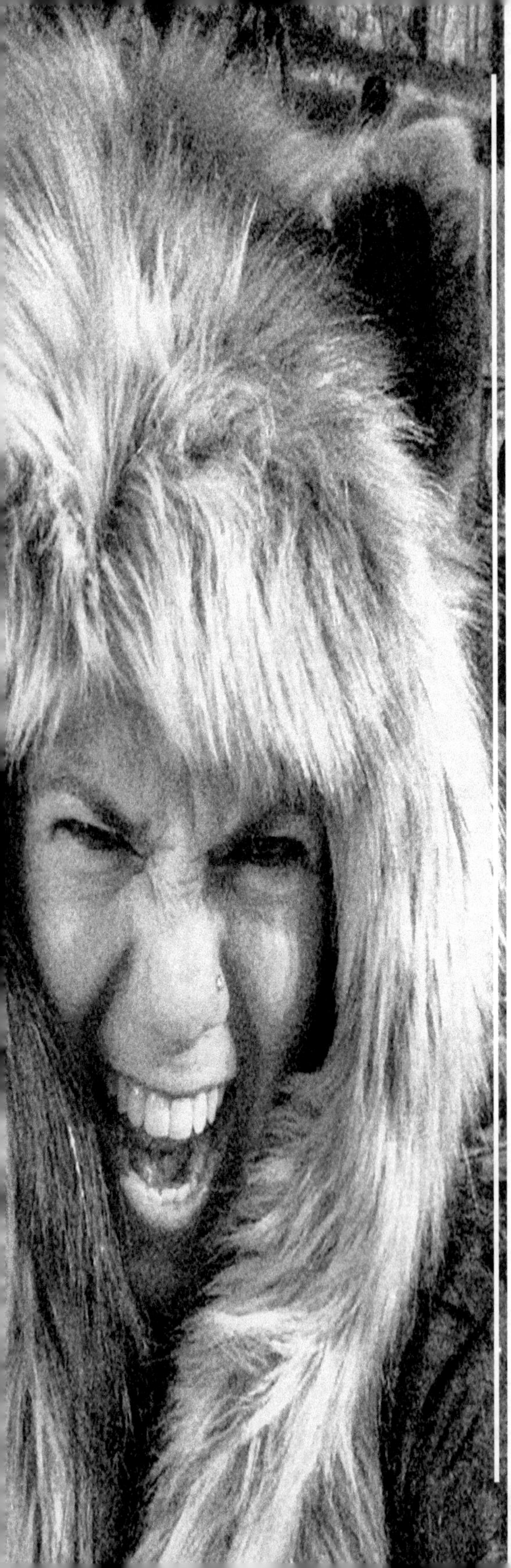

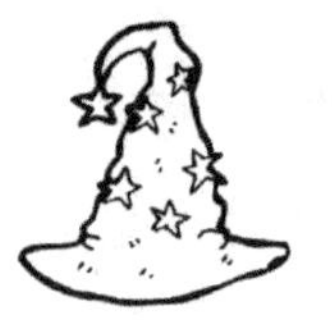

Grey wolf

I am a

grey wolf

fiercely loyal

to those I love

wild

free

spirit

Reach

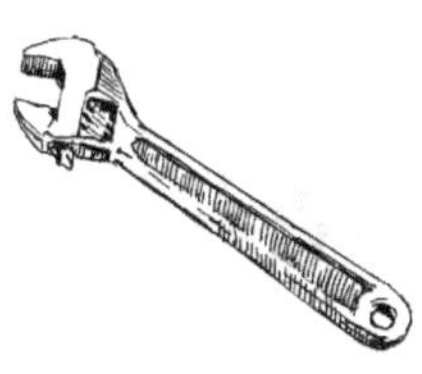

nothing
is out of reach
all
that's needed
is
a taller ladder
or
a bigger
softer heart

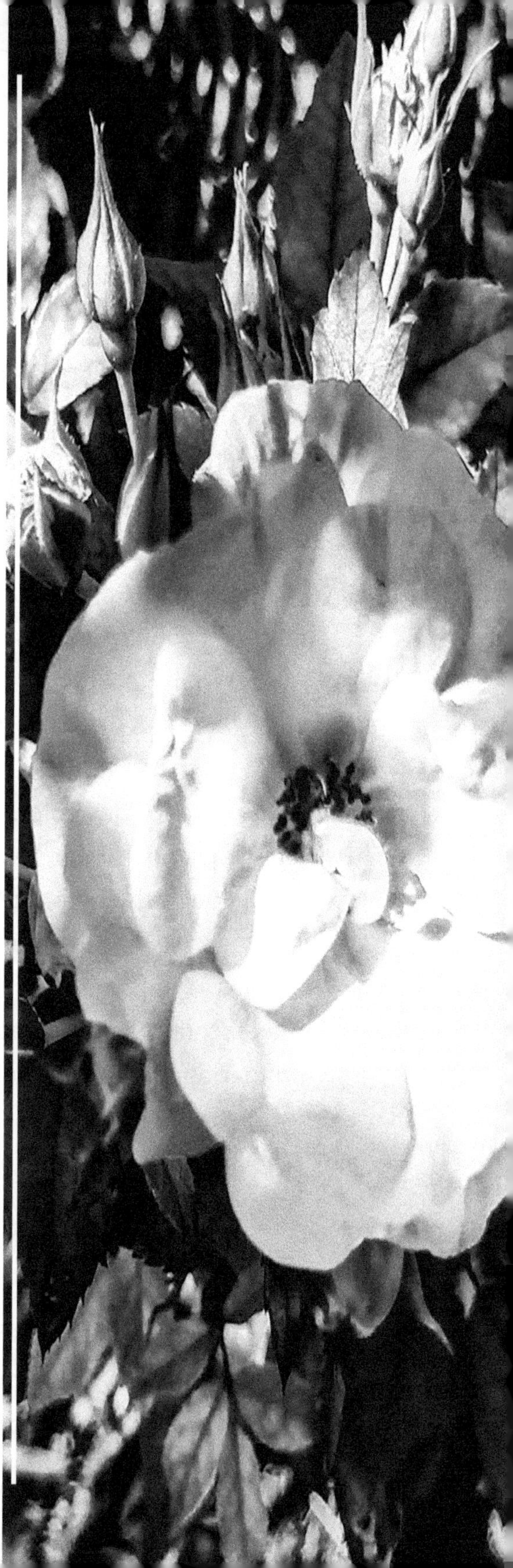

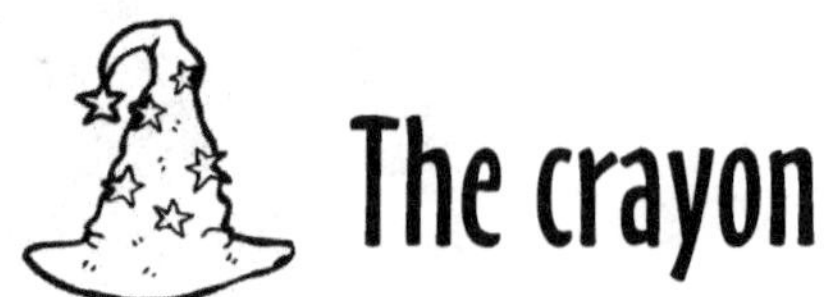

The crayon

The Crayon named Flesh didn't necessarily look like me

Early on I switched to Cerulean, Sea Mist and Violet
To describe my true colors

Thank you Vincent Van Gogh for showing me the Fauvist groove
And thank you Crayola for having the wisdom to admit
What's in a name?
A Crayon is just a Crayon

So Flesh became Peach and colors that I knew and loved
Mahogany and Apricot, Raw Sienna and Burnt Orange
Found their way out of the sixty-four pack
And into a multicultural meeting of the tribes

I once had a teacher tell me to pour out all of my crayons onto my desk
And tear off all of the paper wrappers

He said, "The words will just confuse you."

And so I learned to feel all of the colors and blend them together

Last night I had a dream
That in my hands I held Crayons the colors of people
And I was tearing off the labels

Games of chance

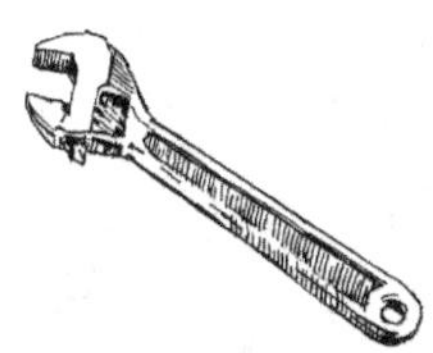

You play
a
game
you
lose

leave the midway
while you
still
got
subway fare

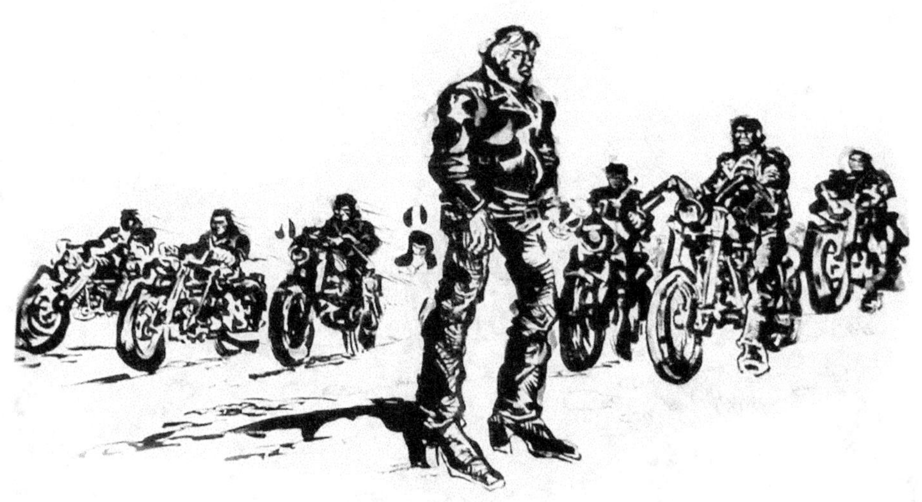

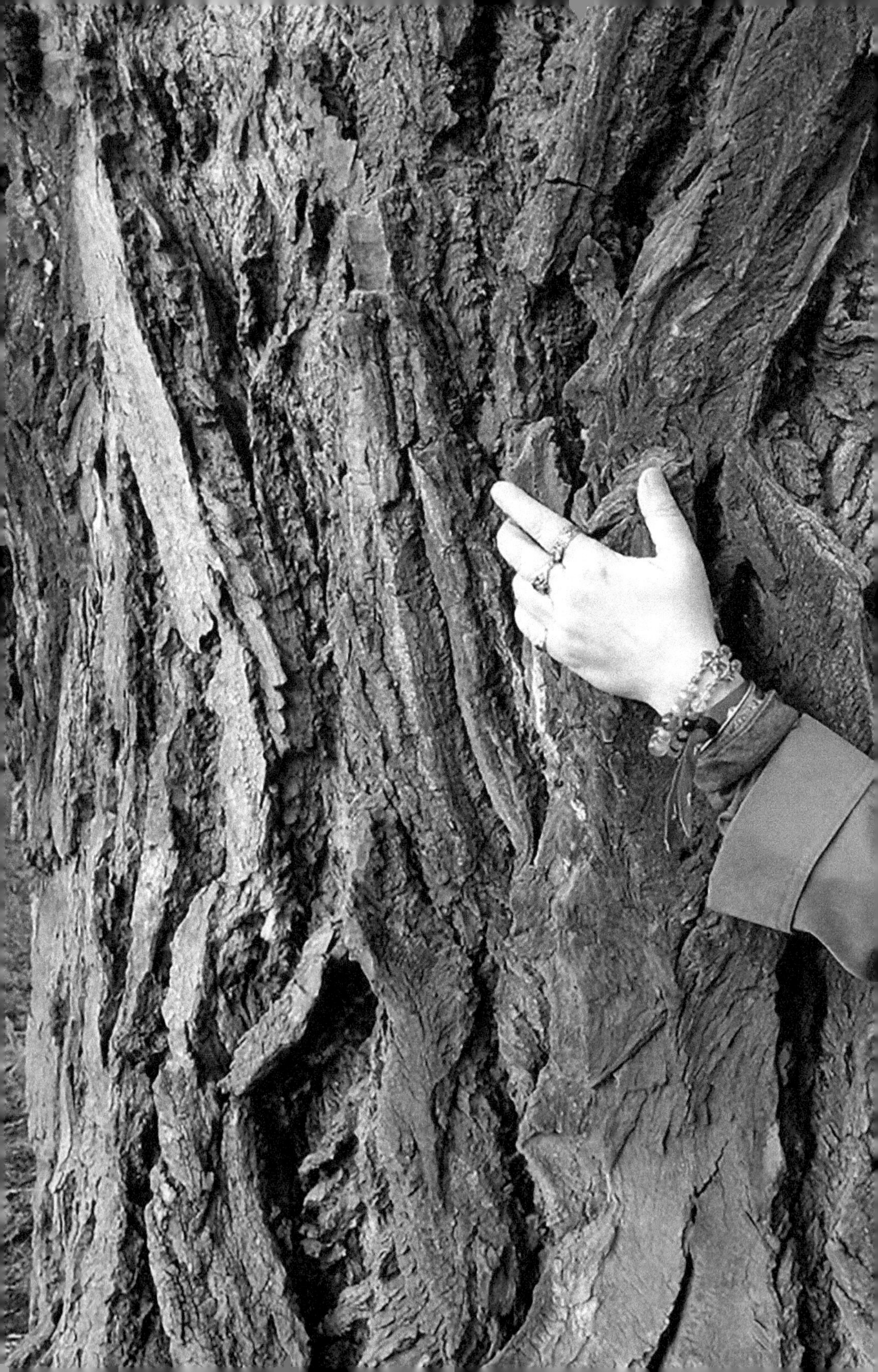

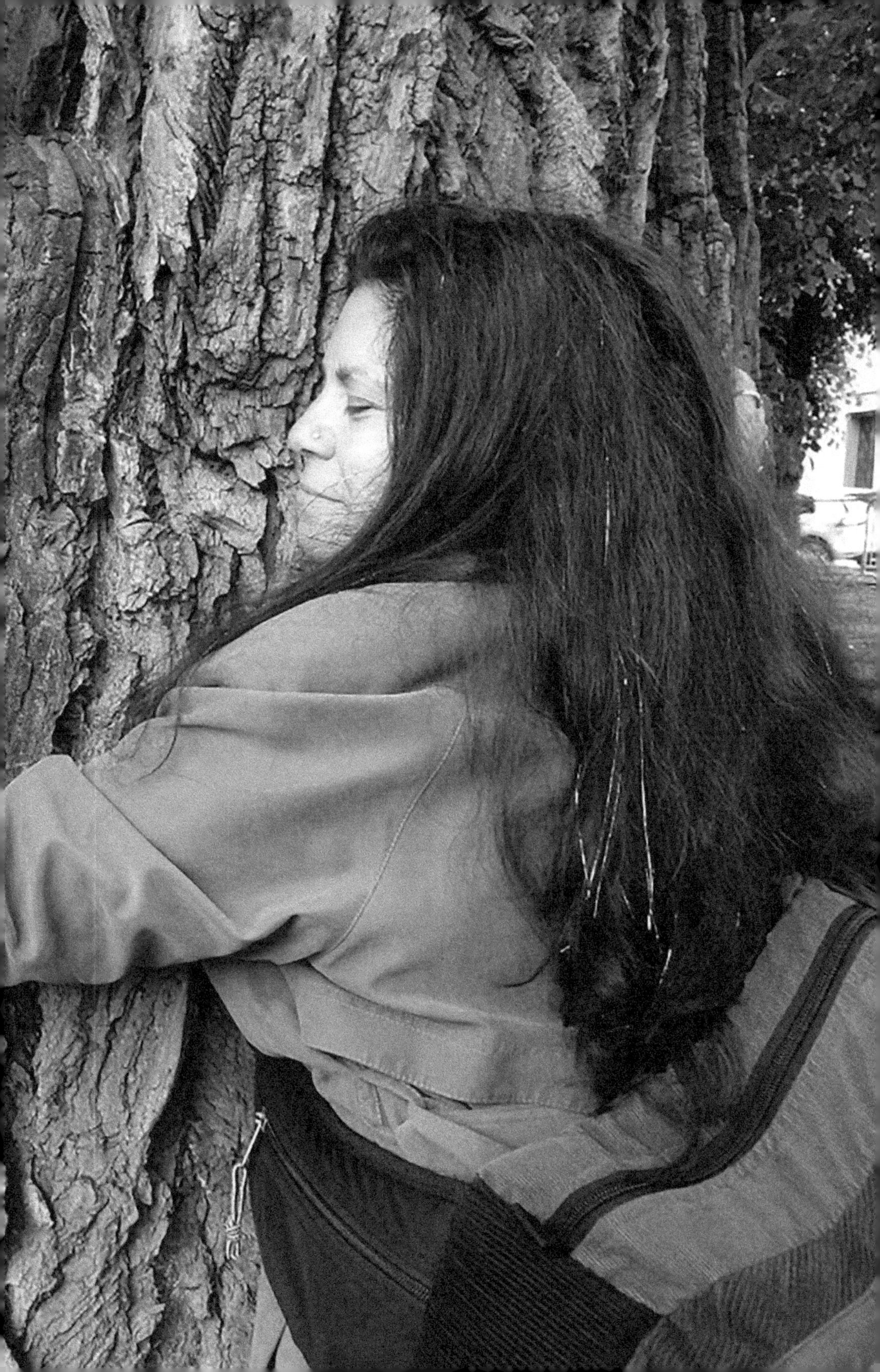

Waiting for you

Have you found a flesh robe?
If not
the joke's on me
dragon breathing fantasies
snake venom
painting patterns
tattooed
on what
I'm yet to be

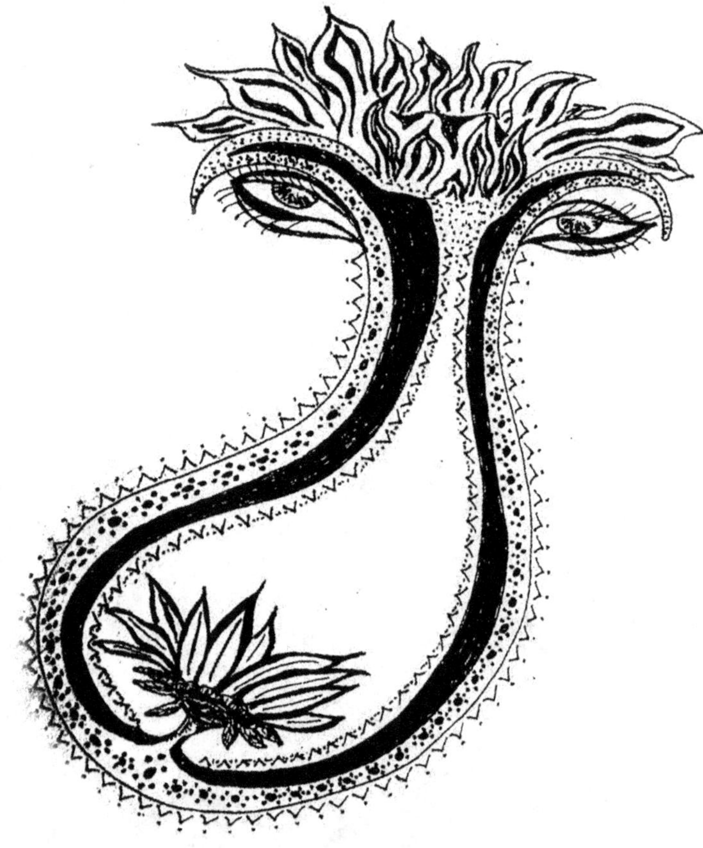

Dominic Albanese *Ambika Devi*

Last night

Last night
in the
in and out
of a thunderstorm
in the
in and out
of a love affair
distance only not ending or
over “only just begun.”

Speaking hush
whisper cuddle,
“You are the reason fruit stays
juicy.”

Hold my hand
roam moan rub slide up down
all around

then
my empty bed
was less “empty”
fluff up the pillow
she would have used
tuck sheets freshly washed

other rooms ... all quiet
said words to begin dream

of both of us
far away
but entwined ... spoon to spoon

a dark night not a hint
of gloom

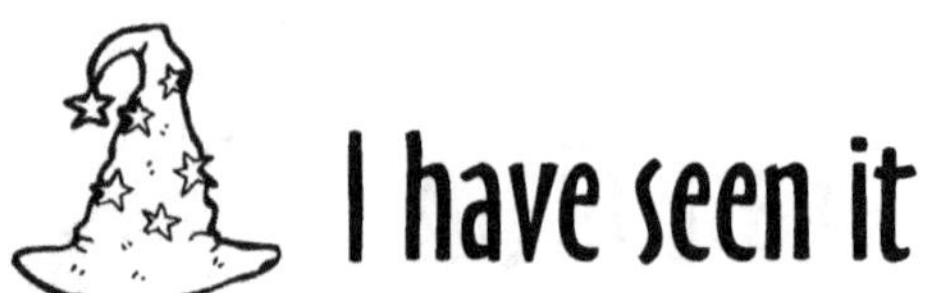

I have seen it

I asked her if she believes in God and she answered "No,"
the expression on her face begged for why

and I continued

what about nature
and the force of energy in everything
from the wind to a quark

what about digestion and lightning
what makes your eyes blink
this is proof
the force that resides in everything
It does not have gender or color
But it exists

She blinked

What makes us grow or die or love?
No answer

Perhaps I cannot change
the hearts and minds
of everyone
but I feel your presence
and love
in everything
everywhere

omnificent
Eternal
I see you

Some days

Some days
it is all
I
can do
sit on the porch
watch
soft south wind
wave palm tree branches
see birds fly by
so busy
quick
be still
pray breathe
be still
that after
the bumpy road
my life has been
is
plenty

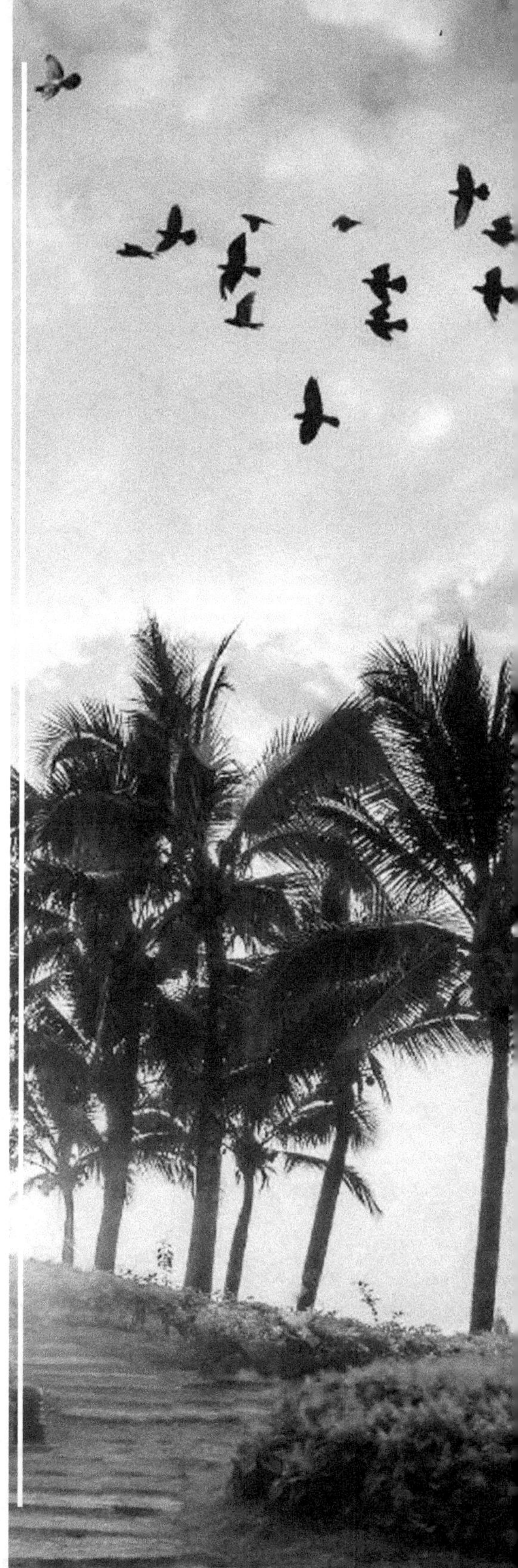

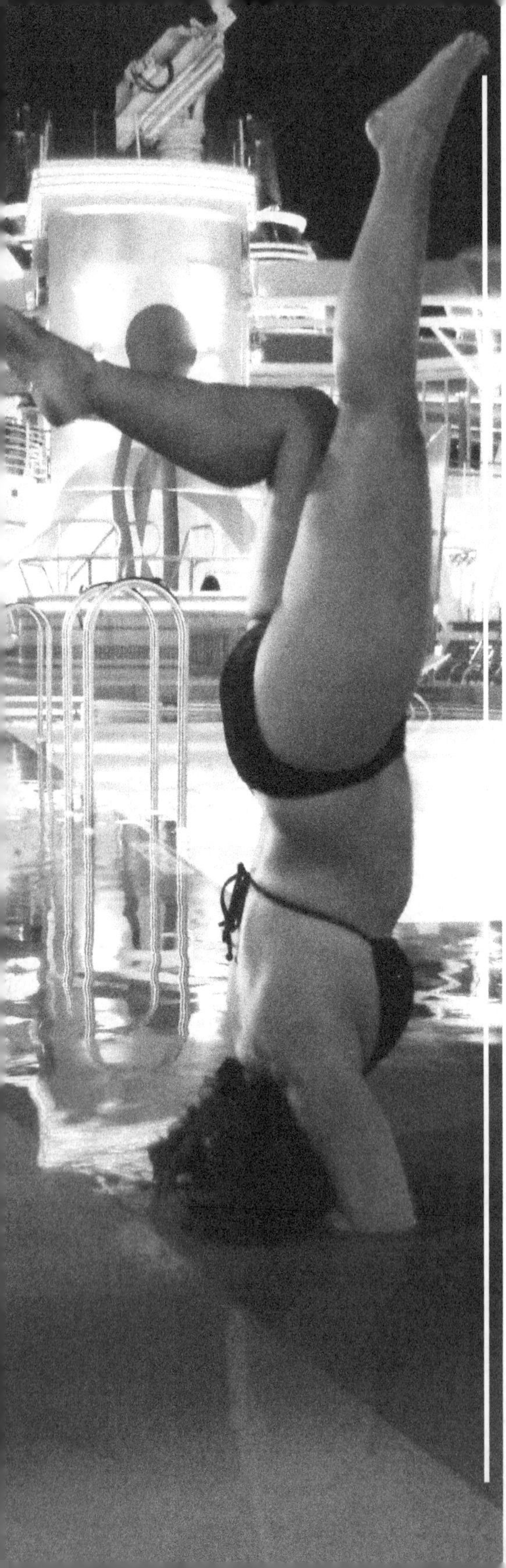

Head stand

Watching people walk
while I'm standing on my head
changes the feel
and rhythm
they bounce and bobble
toy boats
uncertain waters
sailing on
silky satin

Fenceline mindscape

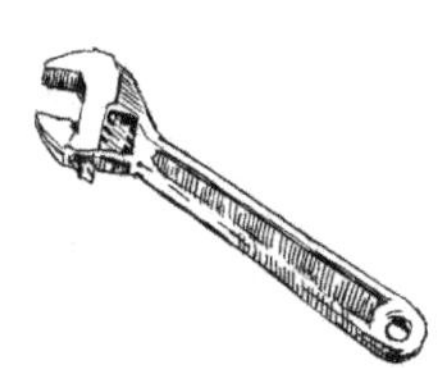

even
in the most
glorious of gardens
nightshade
hemlock
entwine
among
roses
lavender sweet words
sent or spoken

color
vibrancy
vines tangle
from
innocent
dual sided
as is love

thinking
reading
writing
there is always
a hidden danger

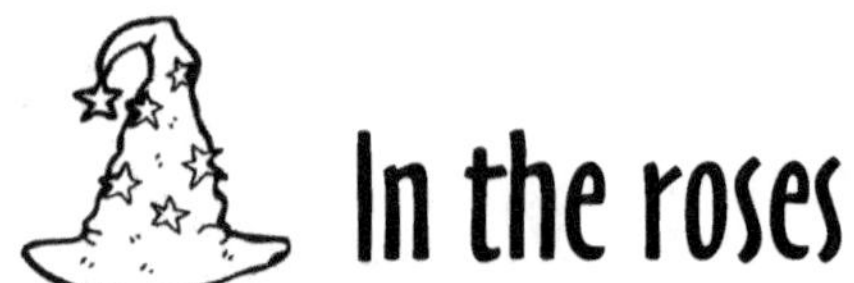

In the roses

This morning I heard your whisper in the roses
and I saw your smile
in the echoing patterns of the petals
I need no reassurance
to know how much you love me
we go beyond the boundaries
of so many years and lifetimes
the leaves are releasing
and as each one dances to its resting place
I am reminded of just how easy it is
for me to let go when we are together

In your eyes I experience all the scenery
we are native warriors
dancing and playing our drums
around a fire

Inside a hut by the ocean
palm trees and hibiscus
a cooking pot bubbling
you are soothing me with your touch

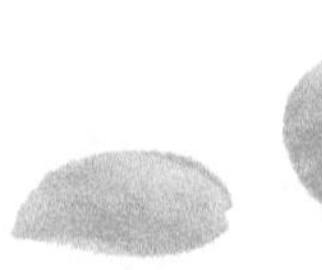

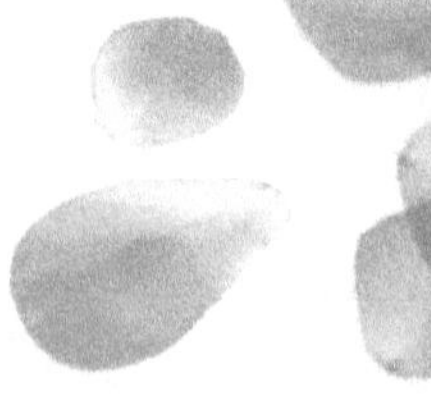

Upon a flat-top pyramid
a great ritual
for which you are preparing me

A falcon flies above he cries, "All is love, all is sacred"

This morning the raindrops fell from the sky
caressing the roses
and I felt your hand brush my cheek

I took petals of the roses
and smoldered them on a charcoal with frankincense, orris, and yarrow
as the essence filled me
I felt your hands on my shoulders
and your breath in my ear

You are always with me
but it is in the roses
that we are eternal

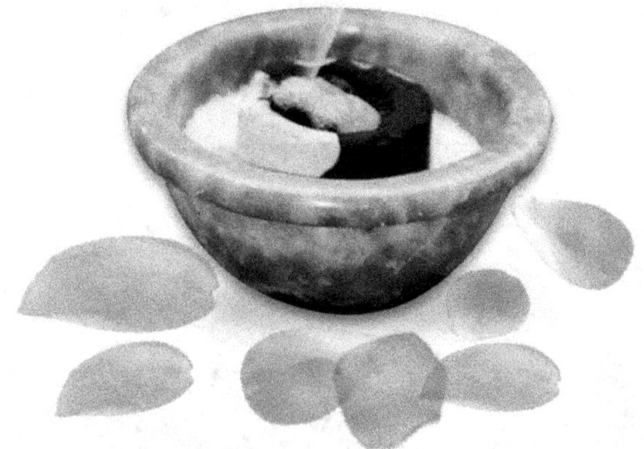

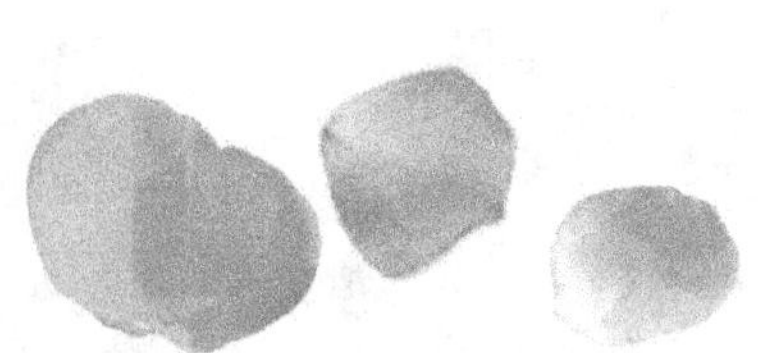

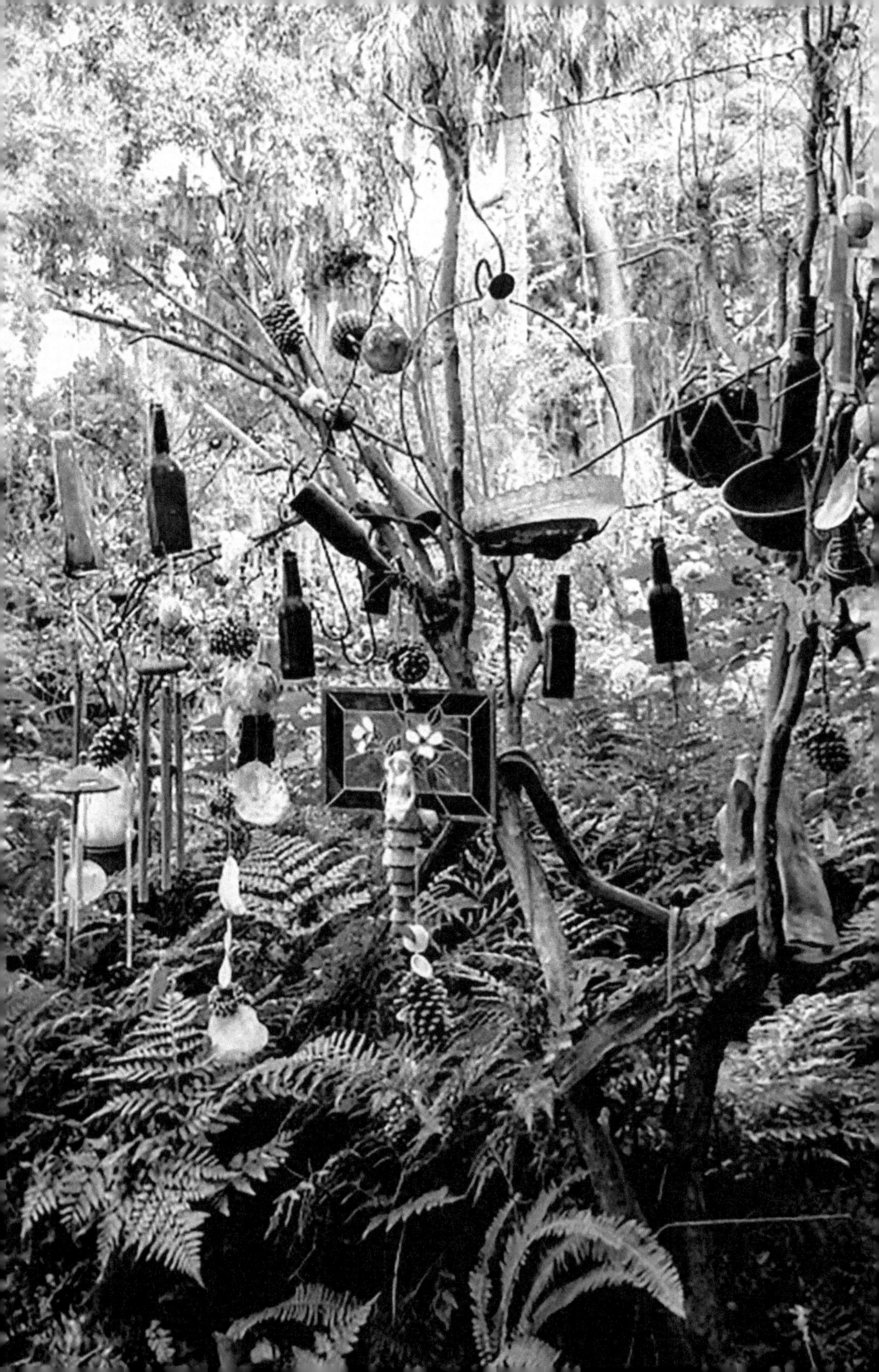

Hummingbird

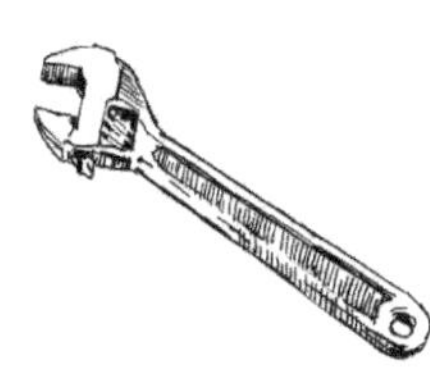

I

am

but a

hummingbird

your

lips

my

red

flower

drink

me

the

nectar

of

you

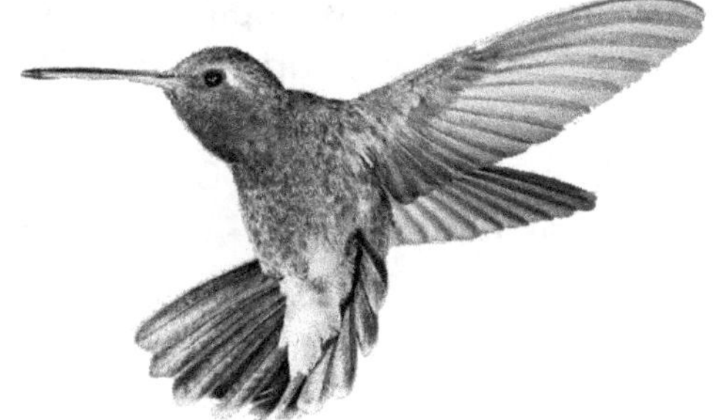

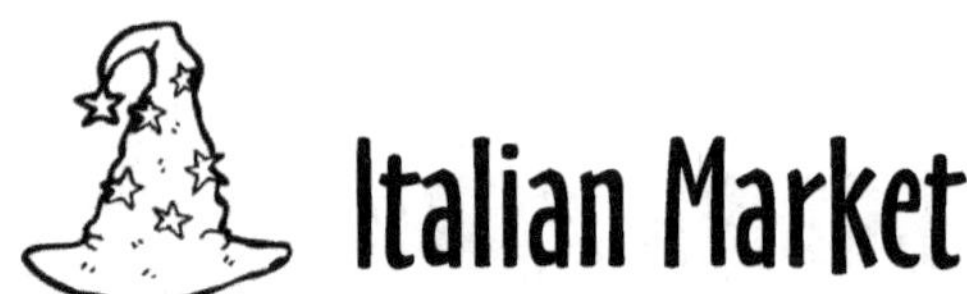

Italian Market

Vinnie, Tony, and Sal are all hanging on the corner tonight.

Nice and warm out, keeps that yellow goo they pass for cheese
nice and liquid on the steaks down at ninth and Passyunk.

My pizzas are staying warm too, as I glide in and out of cars
going my way down a one-way street.

I'm feeling free, got eight wheels on my feet.

Lemon, cherry, watermelon Italian Ice, better than an ocean breeze.
I still can't figure out why those little chunks of fruit tasted so good,
or how they knew just how many seeds to let slide through.

Eels and ravioli, provolone and Stromboli, spice, berries, my sanctuary.

Joey D. Michael T. Frankie Flower,
Did you own anything that wasn't baby blue?

Sitting in your Caddy, sipping espresso, listening to Sinatra
Singing New York, New York

Old-timers playing Bocce, Car Bombs and Corner Shootings,
Taking Sides, Recruiting, Card Games, Running Numbers

Woken from my morning slumbers by the cows across the street
or listening to Anthony's beat as I peeked out the bathroom window and watched him
towel off from his morning shower doing his best Mick Jagger in the mirror
"Start me up, Start me up baby!"

Never had to keep anything in the fridge,
I was living in the moment and you let me.

Sitting on my stoop,
I'm gonna watch the moon hang over Bella Vista tonight.

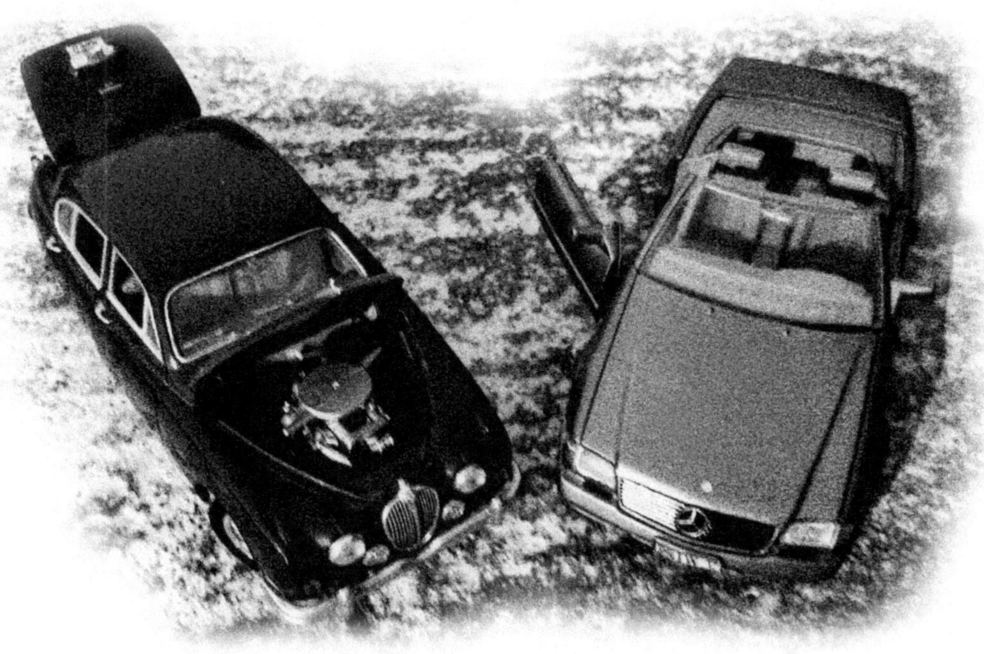

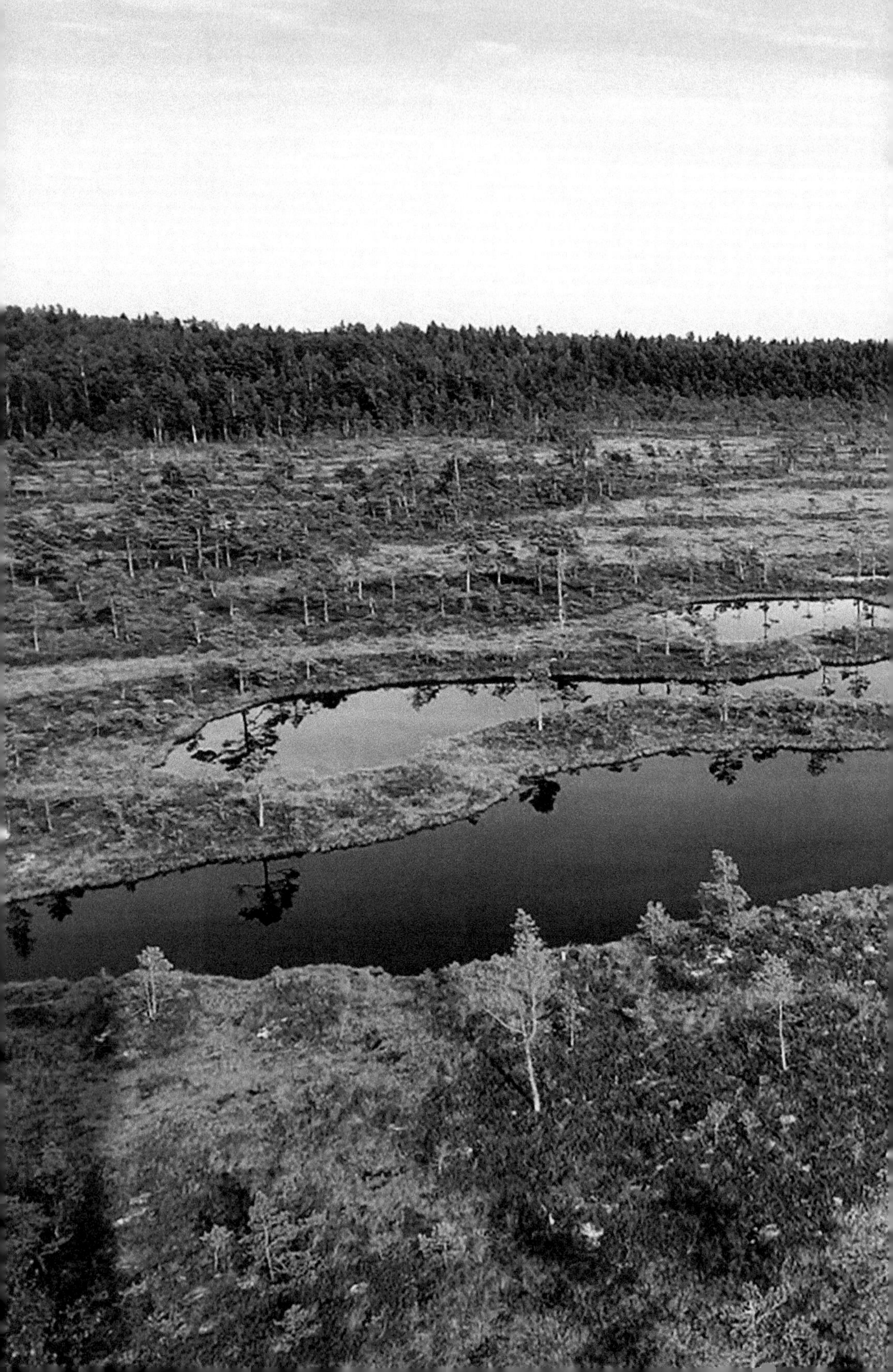

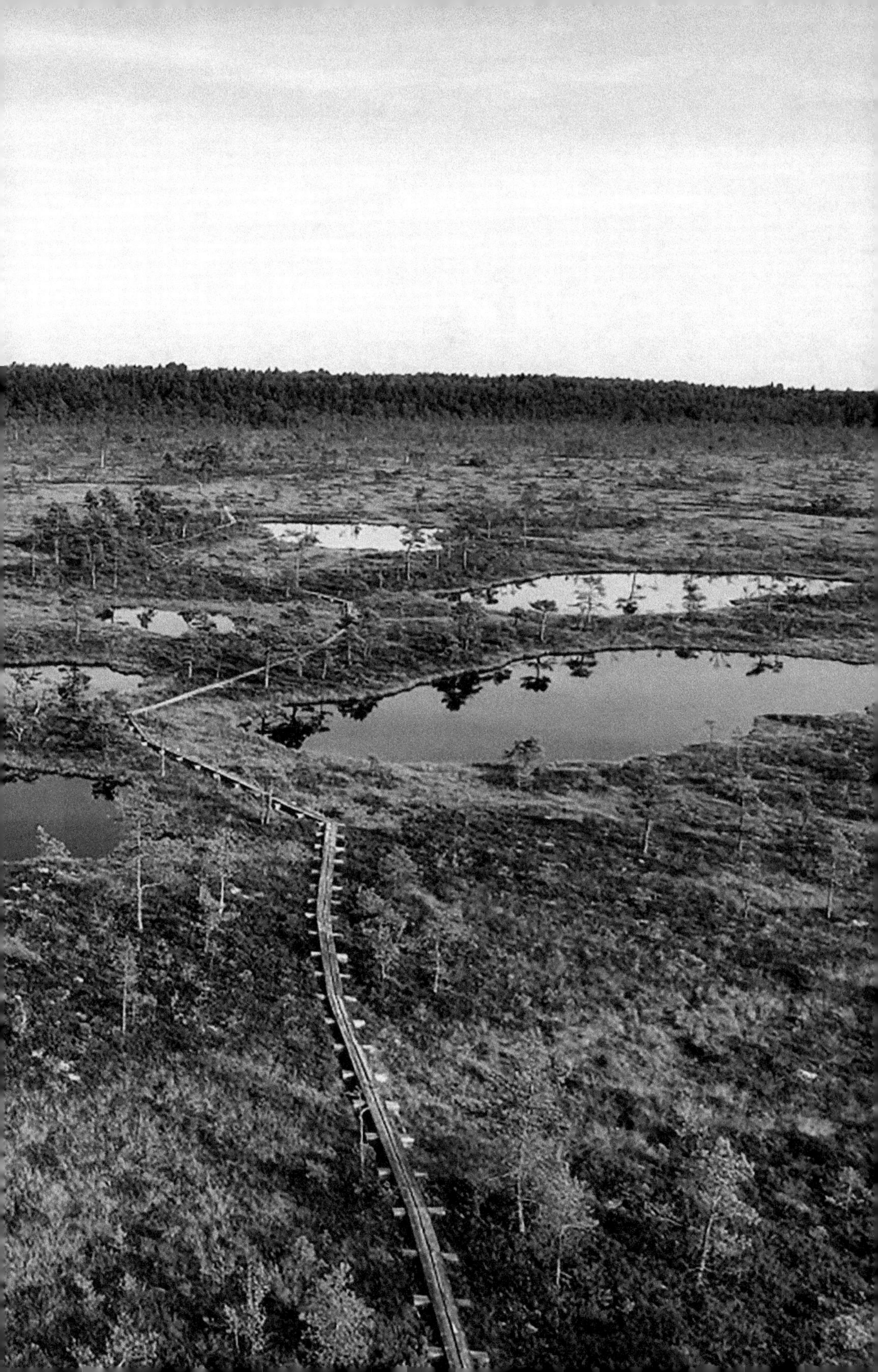

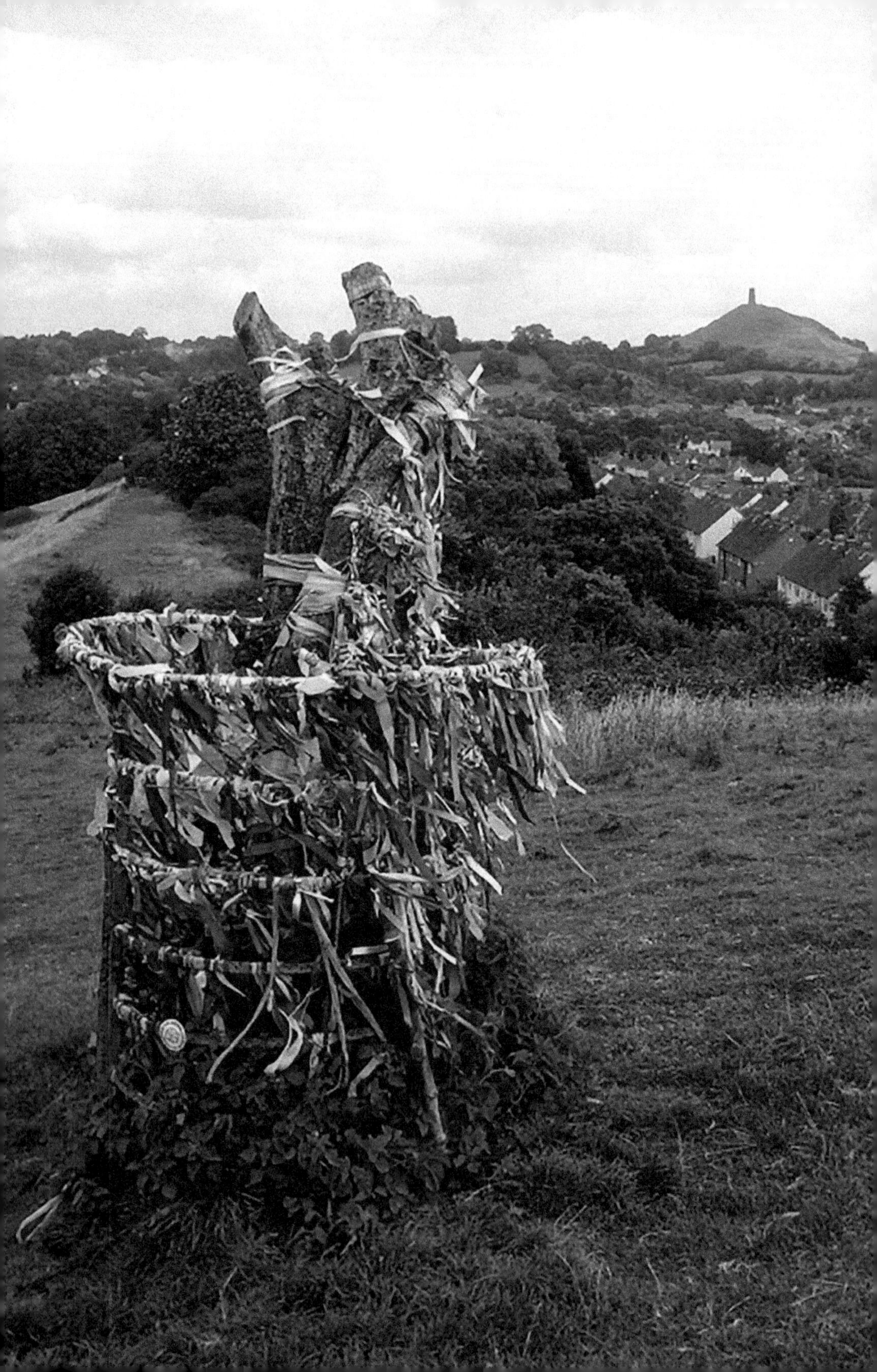

The things we leave

The things we leave
in passing
dishes of good food
kisses
ideas
exchanges
as one life departs
another appears
bringing that memory
food
and kisses along
they made you who you are
now no linger ... fear or ... trepidation
who we knew ... again in passing
carried like treasure chests
not
dragged along in a trailer
we know each other by
sorrow sometimes
by joy
another

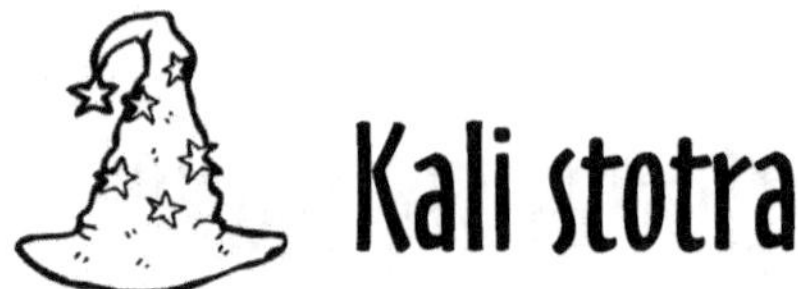

Kali stotra

love daughter
delicious dreaming vision
blaze angel of power
awake in the vast void
speak essential
through ferocious lips
changing woman
of a thousand perfumed colors
melt the naked moon
with deep honey breath
and a symphony
of translucent secret flowers
together we dance
in velvety rhythm
devouring in sacrifice
weak-tongued
poison-hearted eternity
into your
sacred belly

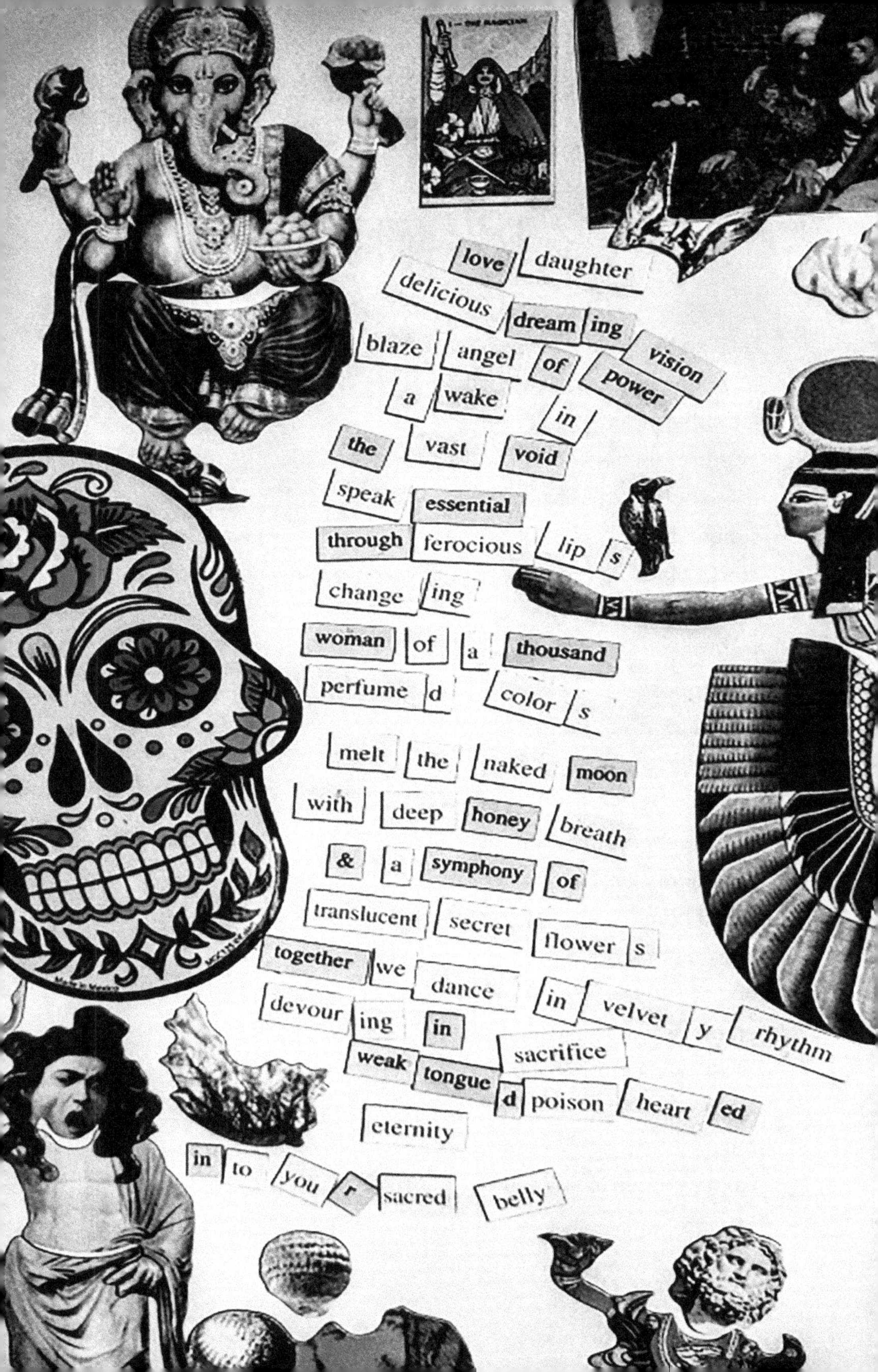
love daughter
delicious dream ing
blaze angel of vision power
a wake in
the vast void
speak essential
through ferocious lip s
change ing
woman of a thousand
perfume d color s
melt the naked moon
with deep honey breath
& a symphony of
translucent secret flower s
together we dance in velvet y rhythm
devour ing in sacrifice
weak tongue d poison heart ed
eternity
in to you r sacred belly

Let's go back

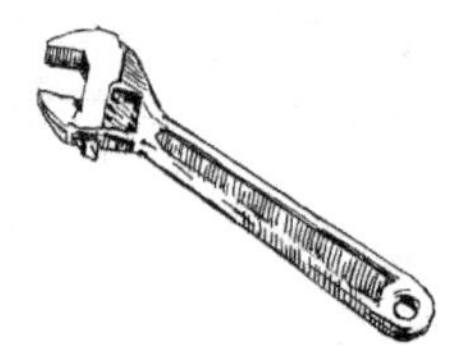

Let's go back
to when we needed each other
for either profit
or entertainment
this whole myth religion
superstitious
cracks black cats Halloween ... to boy-o-boy my new phone is keen
in the end we die
transport
decompose
return to ash or bone
sightless
alone
to the very mother of us all
this spinning rock
called home
does mom scold us
no
embraces us
as all loving mothers do
if
only
we have been loving too

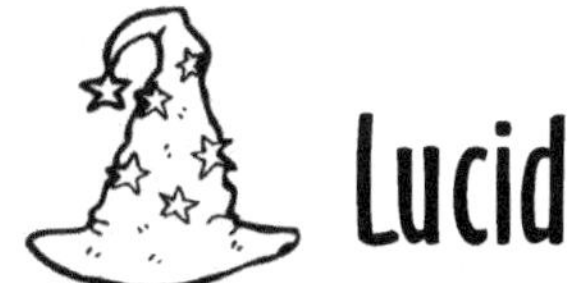

Lucid

Last night I held you
as the chrysalis shattered
then you took wing
flying off into a pale sliver of moon
commonplace cannon shots
muffled conversations
drooling drivel
liquefies and pools
I curl up alone
under a rotting log
to slumber and dream

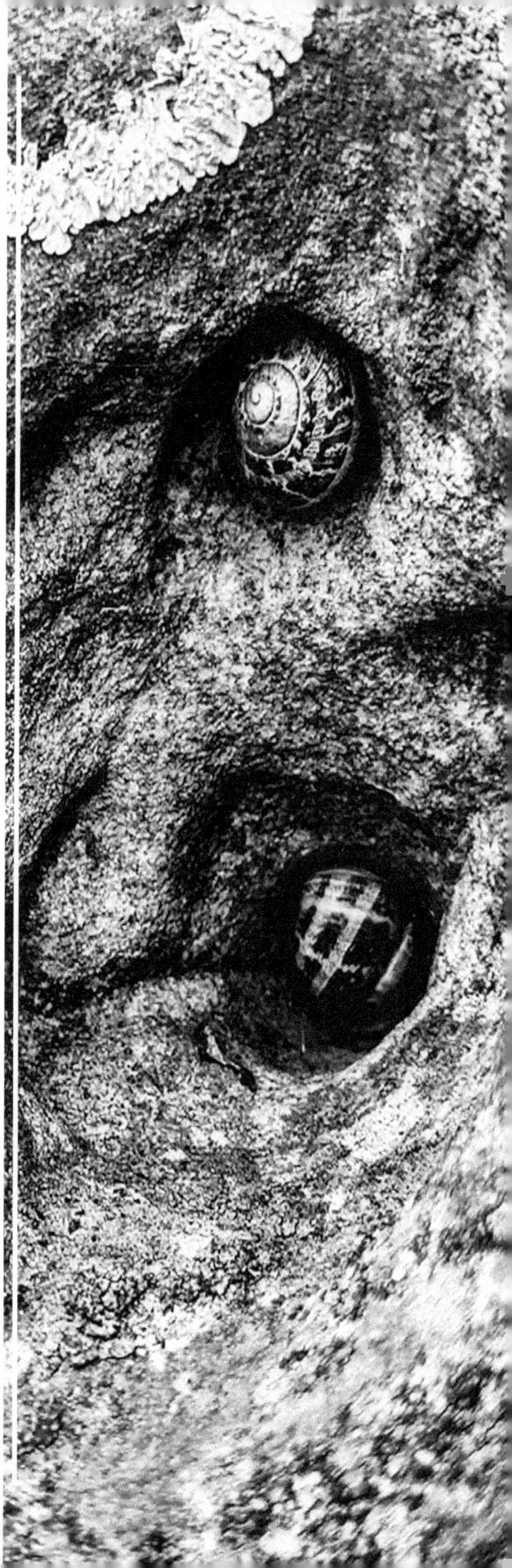

Some

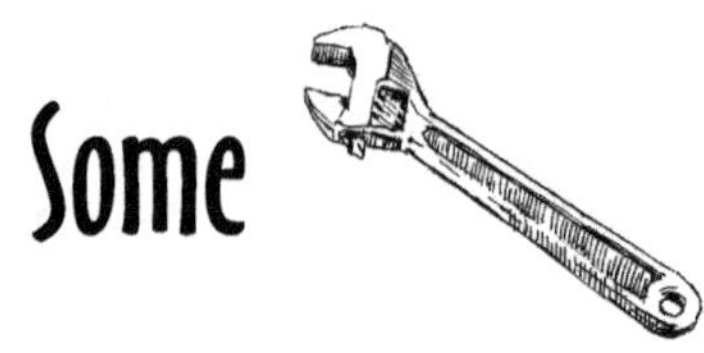

Some will get this
some won't
plastic gauge
oil clearance in
rod bearings
an' crank an assembled
engine over
before ya put the fire to it
assure good oil pressure
is a lot
like making love
no high RPMs till
up to temp
and every moving
part
is
well
lubed ... coast mode
and
then hit the go pedal
home
safe
again

Out to Moon River

I went out to Moon River
the air
acrid
tasting of oysters
and marsh grasses
singing
haunting
spirituals
the mud bade me to wade in the water chil'

Johnny Mercer in my ears
his windswept mystery castle
a dot on the distant horizon

rice chafe falling
like grace and goodness
to the ground
crunching shells
that grind the past to dust
from a secret garden

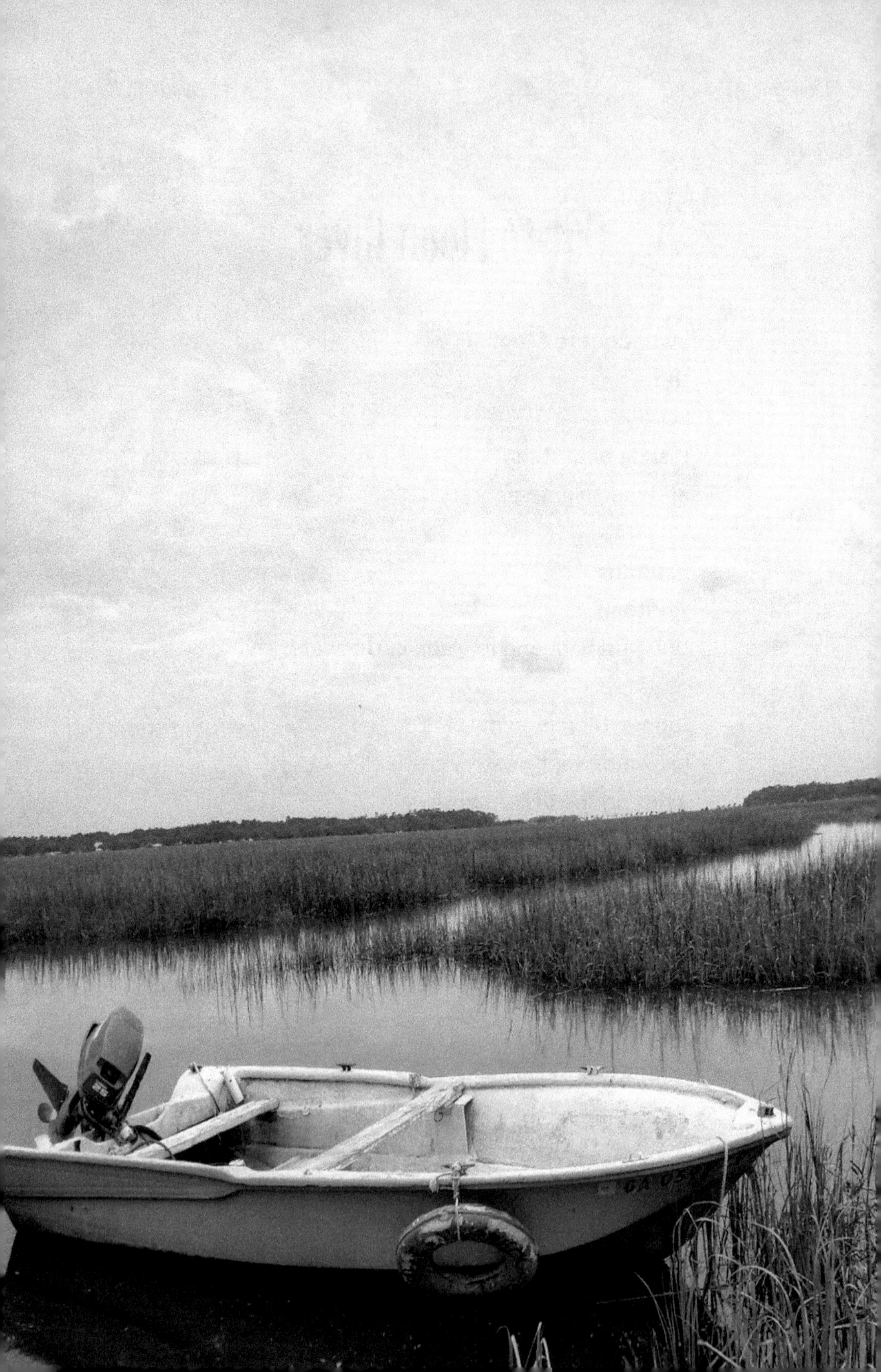

Only the river knows

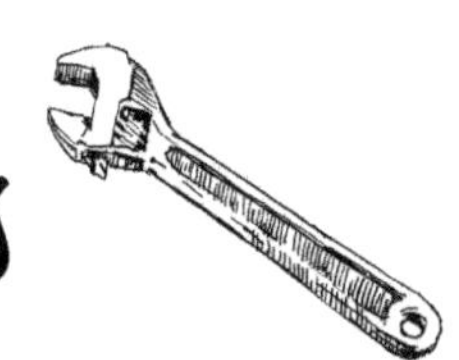

Only the river knows
my secrets
fears
tears
changing moods
paddle grass
flats wonderment
eons
passing tide moving
it never wants
to know me
or care about a lie
I told
or money I stole
or who does
did
or no longer
loves me
never cared for much
other
than a constant inflow
of nutrients ocean born
paddle past sandbar dreams
it is really what it seems
mother sister daughter
or sky
solid ground
in all walking crawling slithering
things
I promise river keeper
vow to
be a better man
river cares not
keep my water clean
so this sandbar dream
flows soon
to return to go on
roll
green mother
of us all

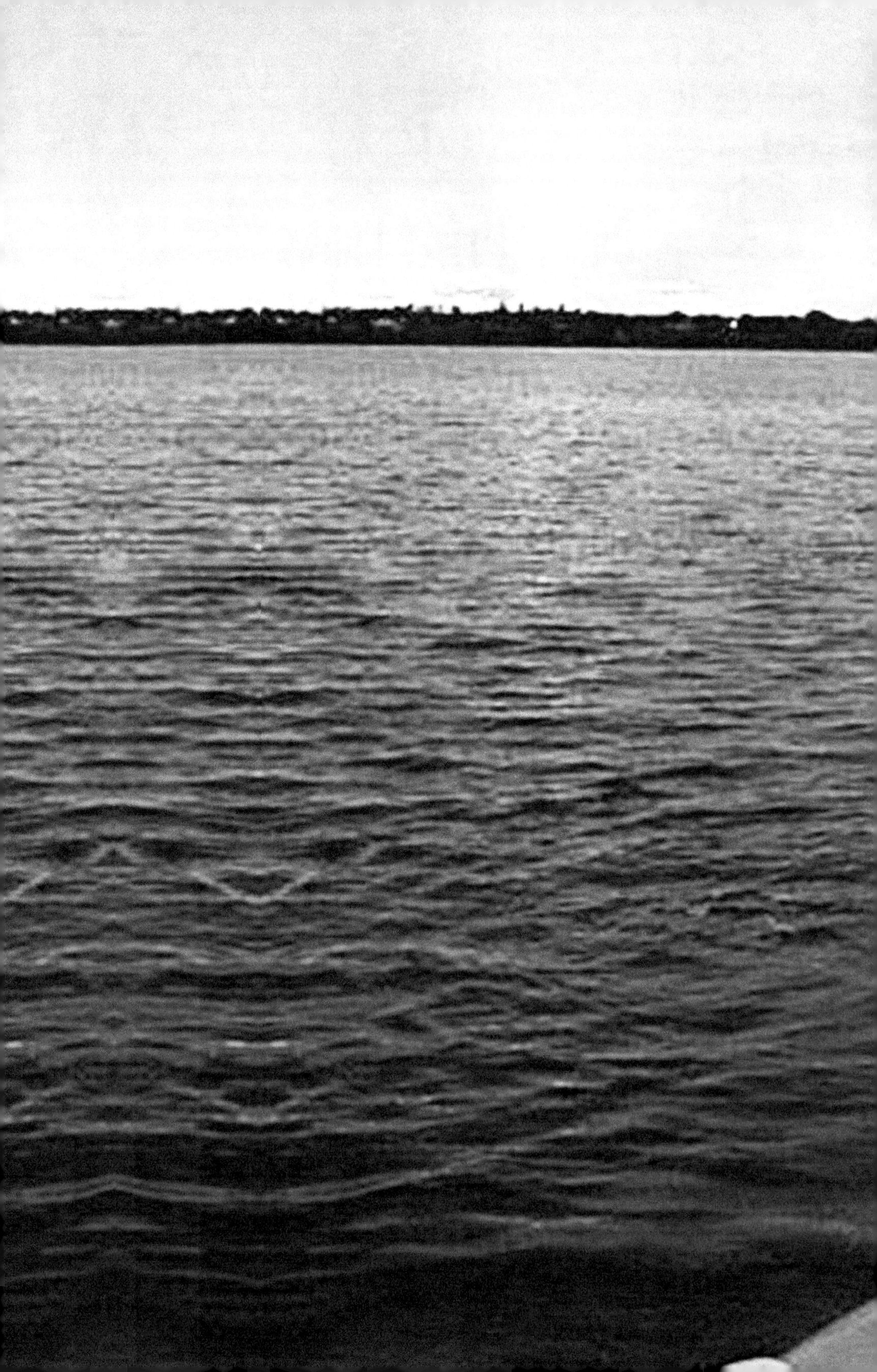

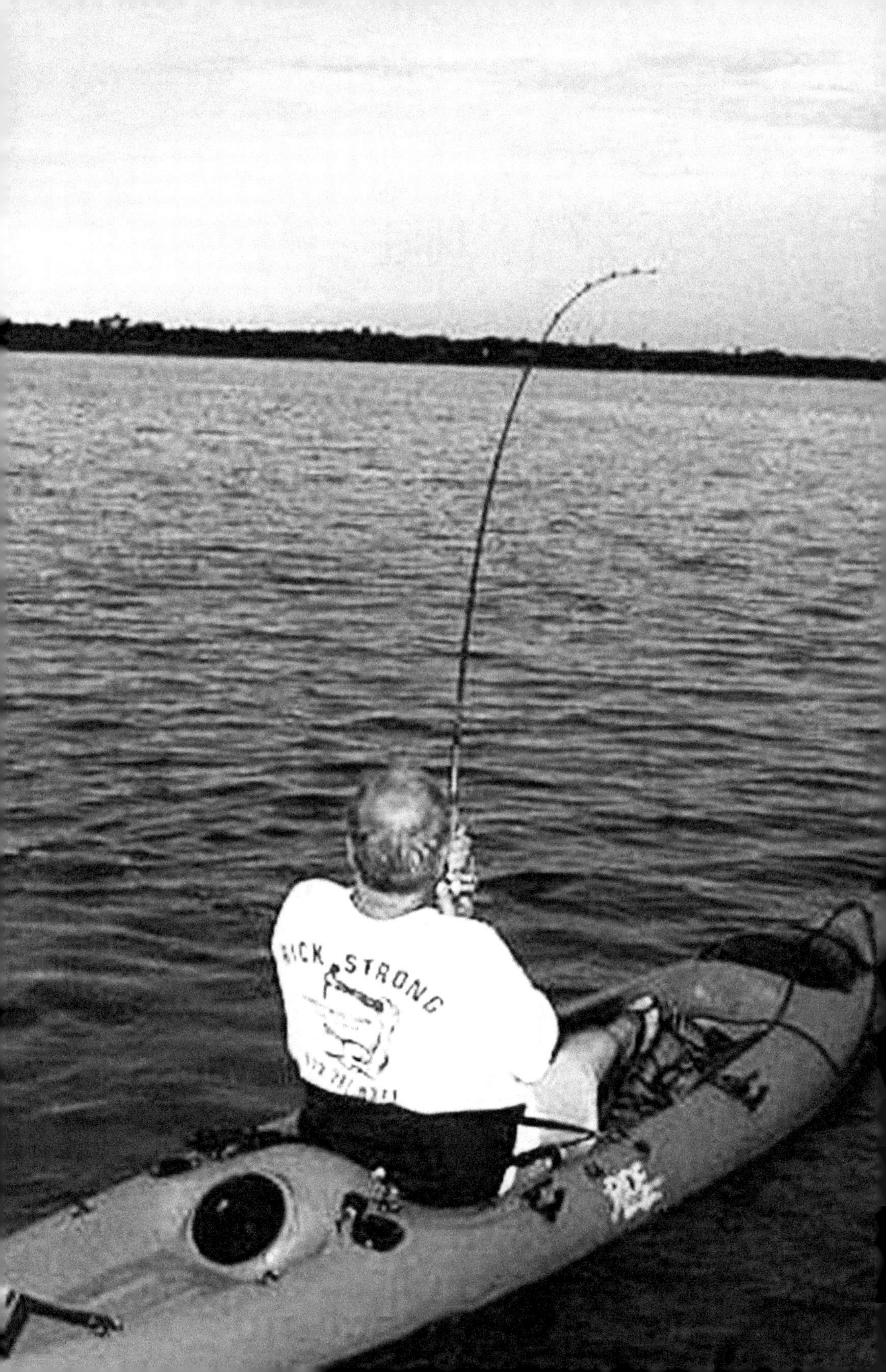
STRONG

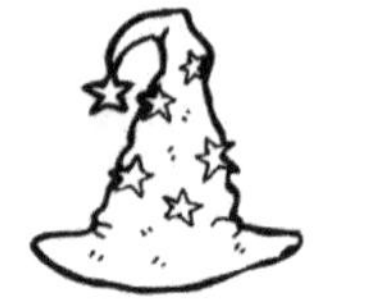

Quiet

I have an ocean of quiet
so silent

I can hear
beyond the light sound of rain falling

through the screened enclosure
onto the surface of the pool

I can hear past the walls
and the jungly woods behind the house

past the main road
almost a mile away

I listen to the clouds
and listen to my breath

quiet

observing
the rhythm

of existence

River dance

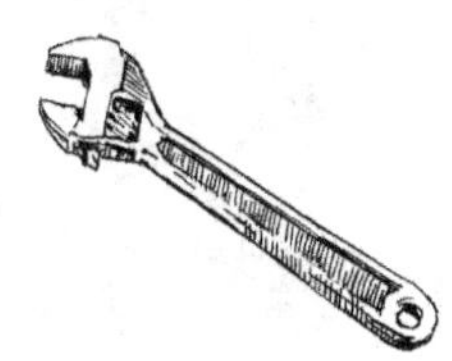

on water
sand bottom
east stem
of
Indian River
shell mound
makers
once
paddled
long canoe paths
I look for signs
of who was here
and see you in the distance
waving
a small hand

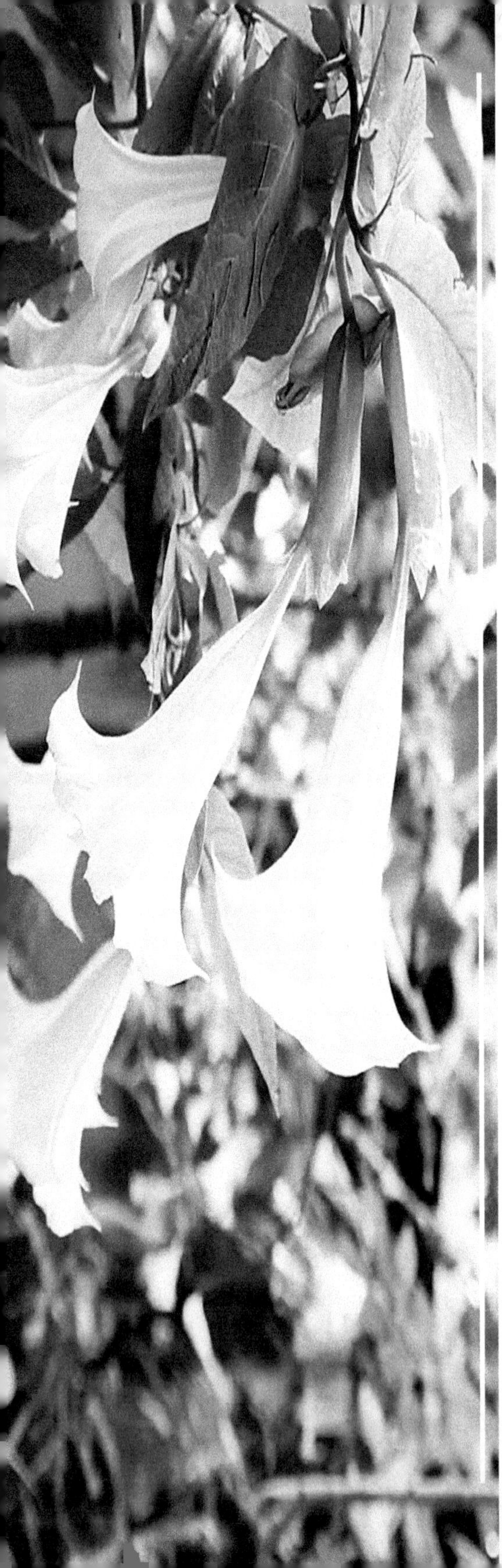

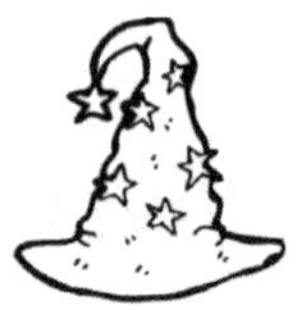

Moon flowers

Moon flowers
telling me tales
of deep-rooted memories

I'm drunk
from a waft
of almost too-sweet Jasmine
plucking a sprig
to decorate my braid
hoping to inhale genius

of words

melody

feeling the counterpoint rhythm
and rhyme
shaking my soul
to awaken

Psycho evaluation

One more time
Not knowing
To laugh or cry
"worst thing you have ever done?"
"best thing you have ever done?"
I answer 'em both the same
"Fall in love with someone"

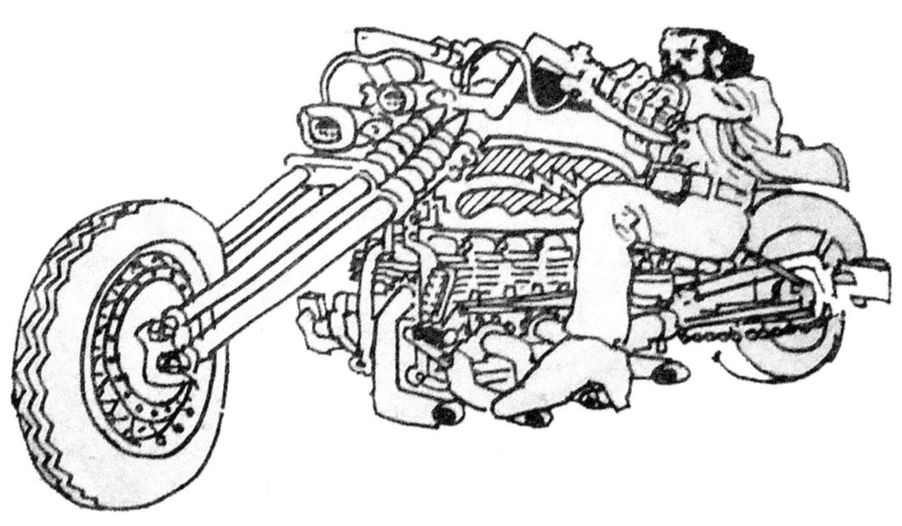

My life as a bee

I remember the hexagonal cells
filled with powders
pale and pure
bright
pungent

cleverly organized by genus and
location
the feel of my tongue drenched in
jelly
fed to me by the devoted

for a fortnight
I fatten
translucent snowy white
no room for us here
in the hive
I have known
all my life

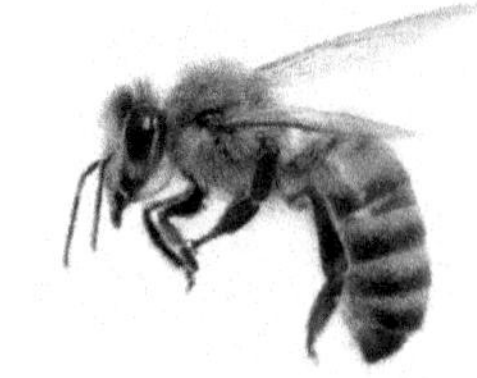

along with my sentries
we take flight
swarm
consecrate

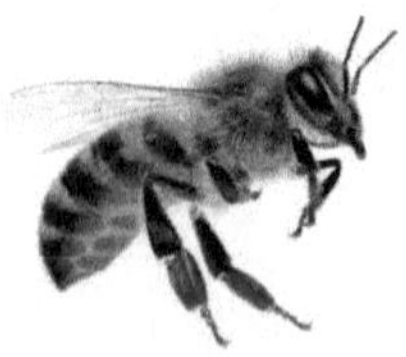

then the beautiful benevolent roar
of a new hive

honey-dripping magic

shiny silken fur flashing

repetition
replication
rifling out
offspring

purposeful

existence

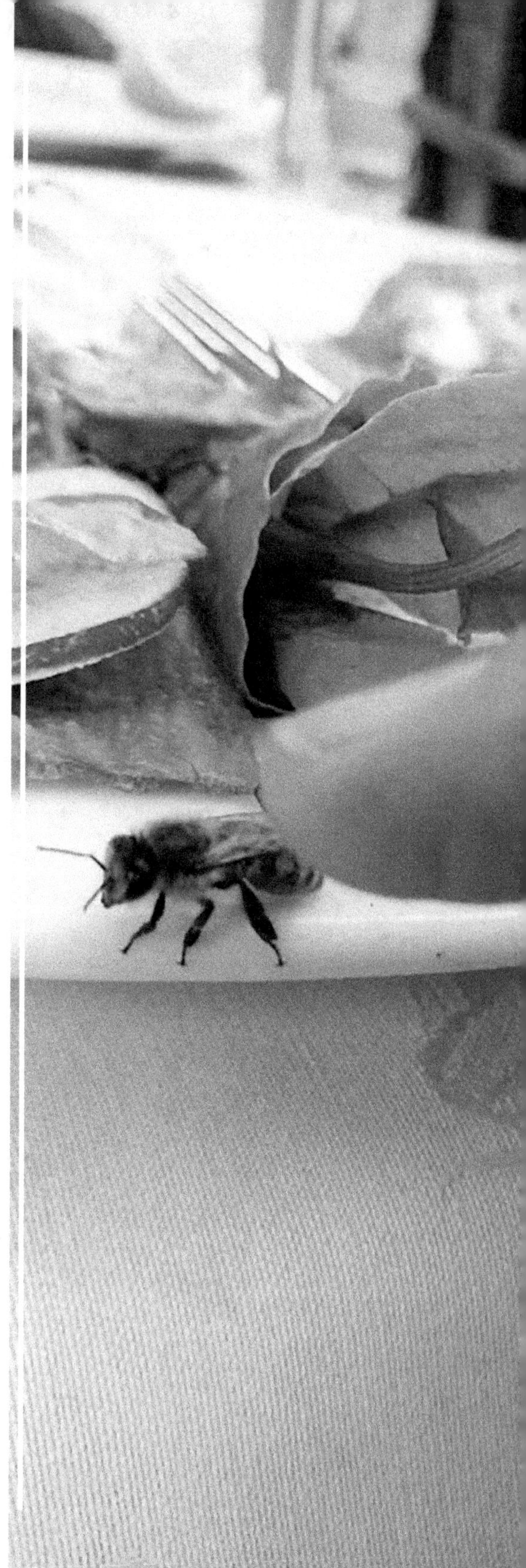

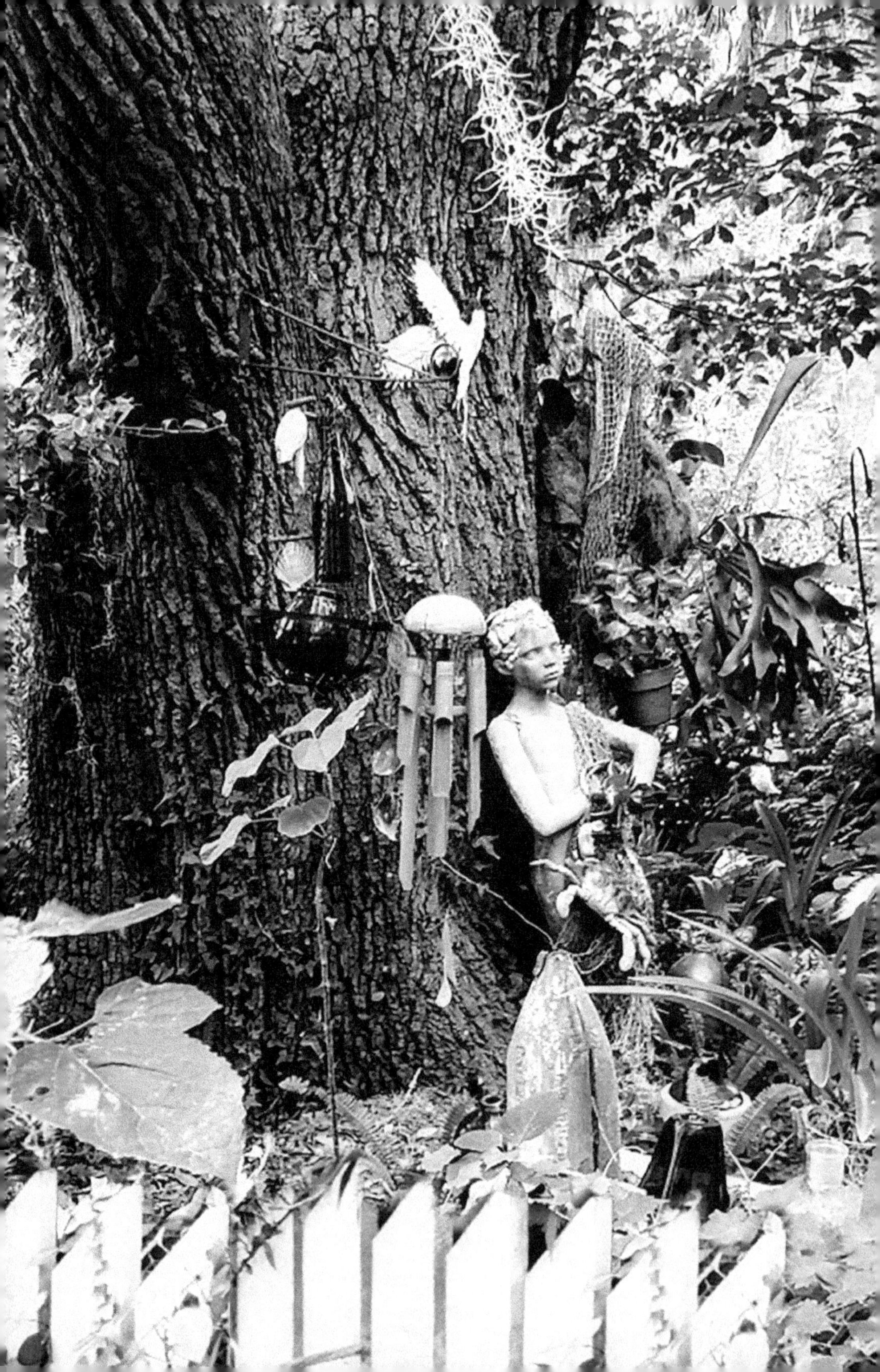

Back fence

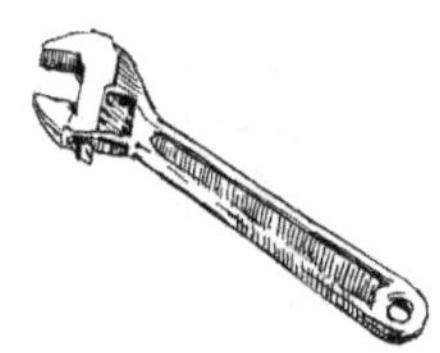

Geometric
spider webs
late
morning glory
entwined
blooming wild orchids
alive
with sparkle
mild shower
rain
memories

Purple petal

Purple petal
still like rain
spring
from over-easy visions
of summer love
and languid smelling
garden gifts

sweet water
playing on your beauty

whispering
white goddesses
moonlike
wintery chant

through the forest
of my dreams

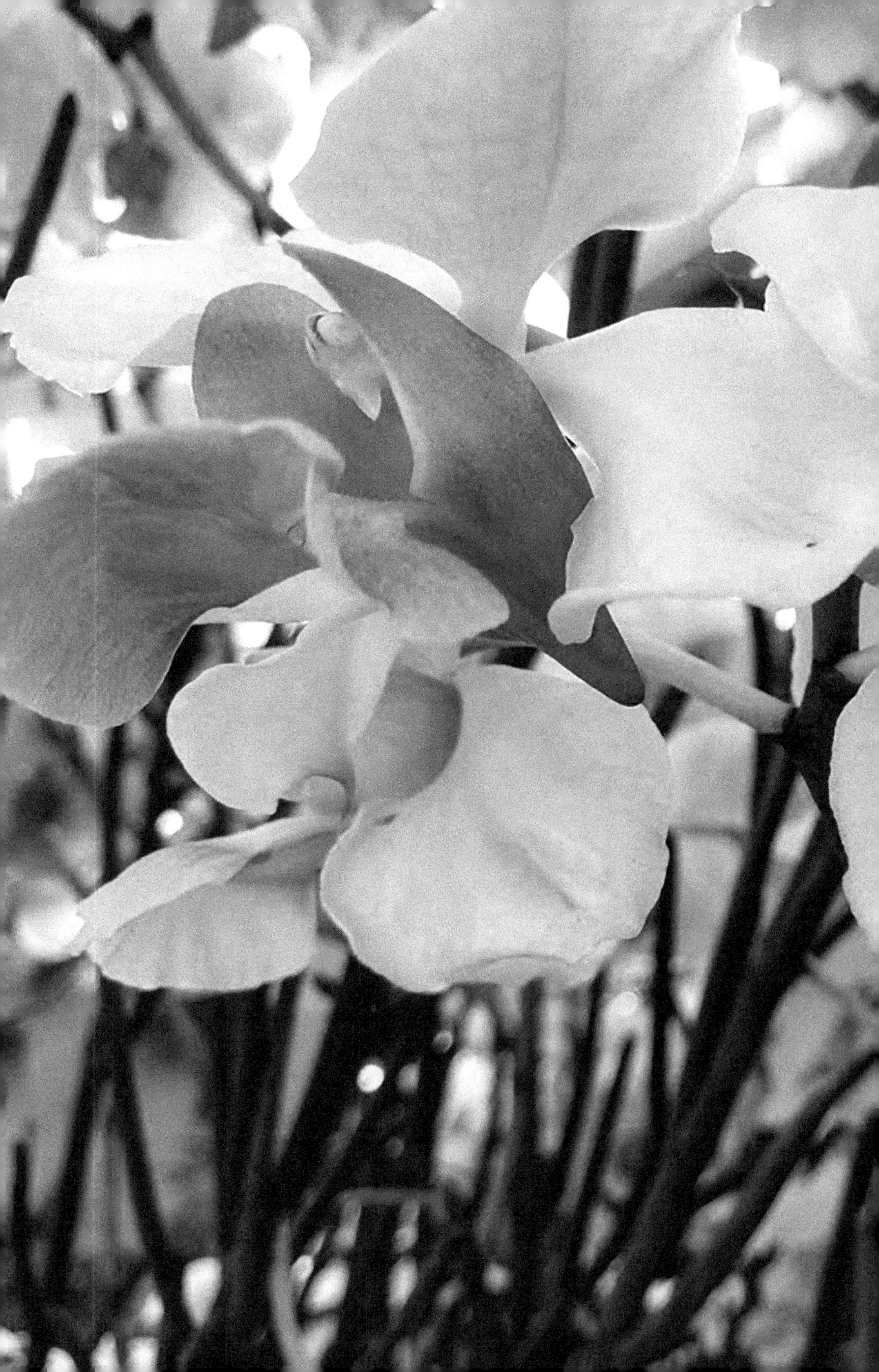

Wondering

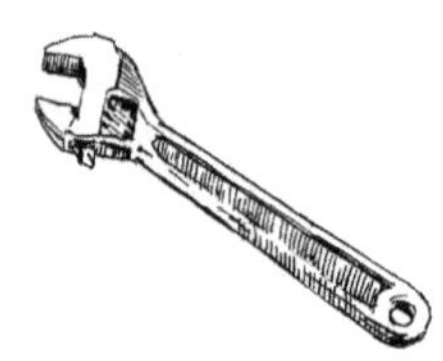

Words
said
in person
airy
conflict or equal
ones
read
alone

trying to sort
meanings
never
printed in any dictionary
or
translated to clarity

brain to heart
heart to brain

some come
loaded
with romance

some
overloaded
with pain

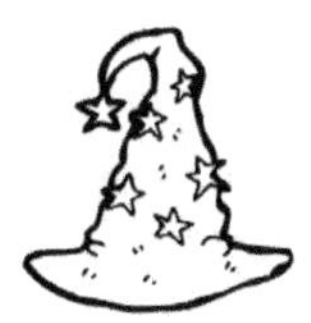

Waiting for you

Have you found a flesh robe?
If not
the joke's on me
dragons breathing
fantasies
snake venom
painting patterns
tattooed
on what
I'm yet to be
most of the time
I'm on the outside looking in
watching you monkeys
climb the walls
puffing chests
look at me
chatter
no thanks
not interesting
nothing to see

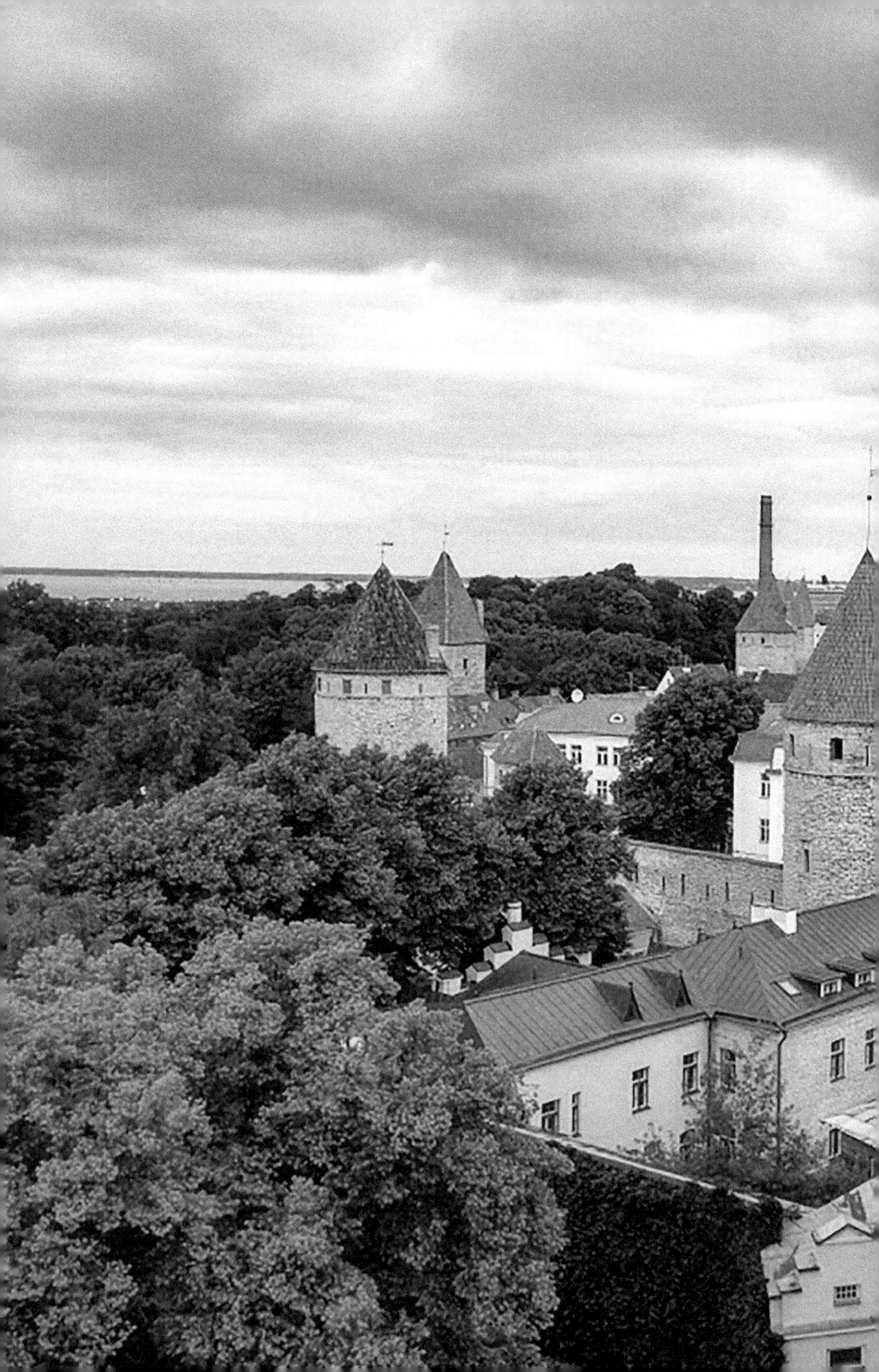

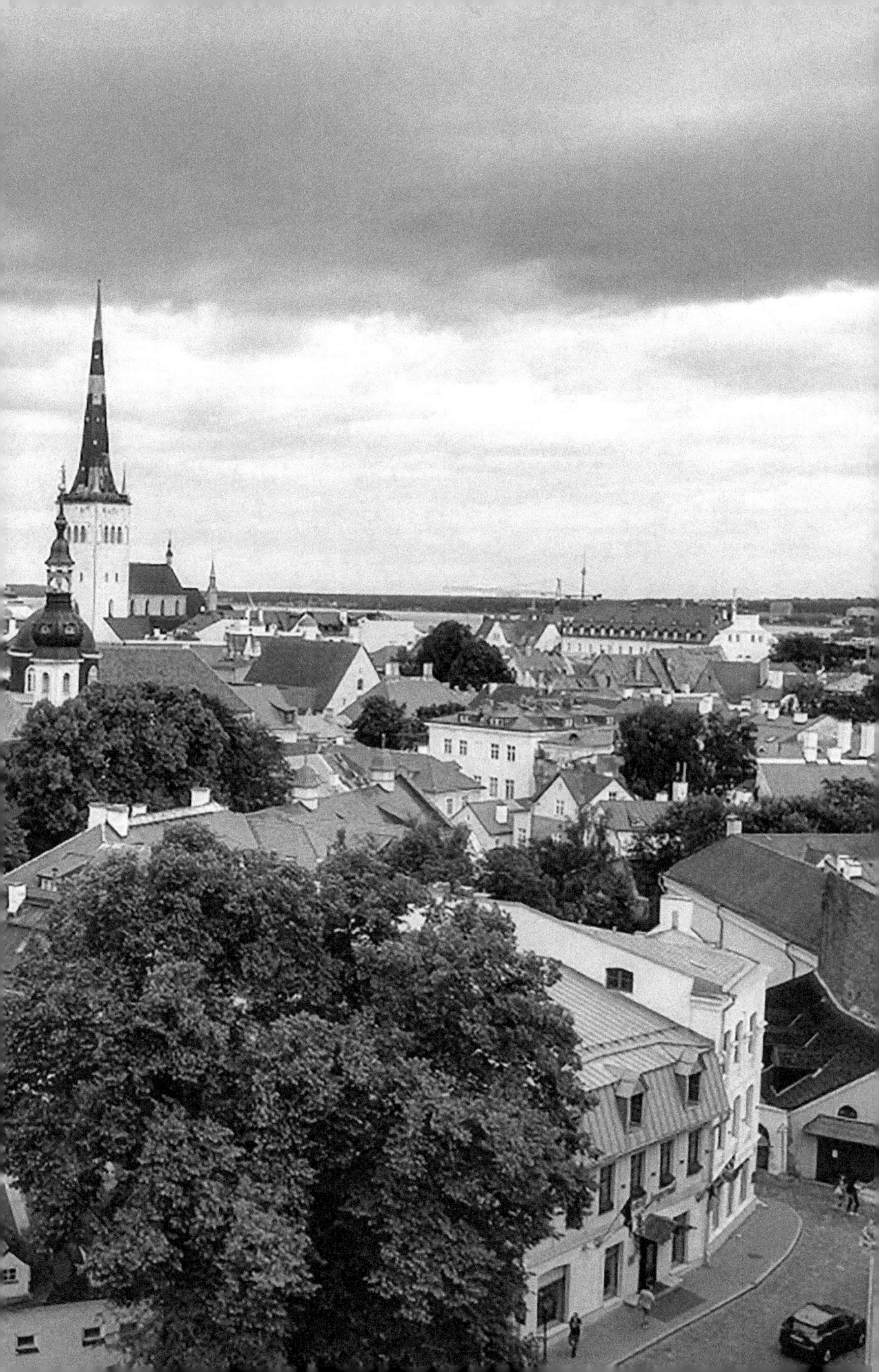

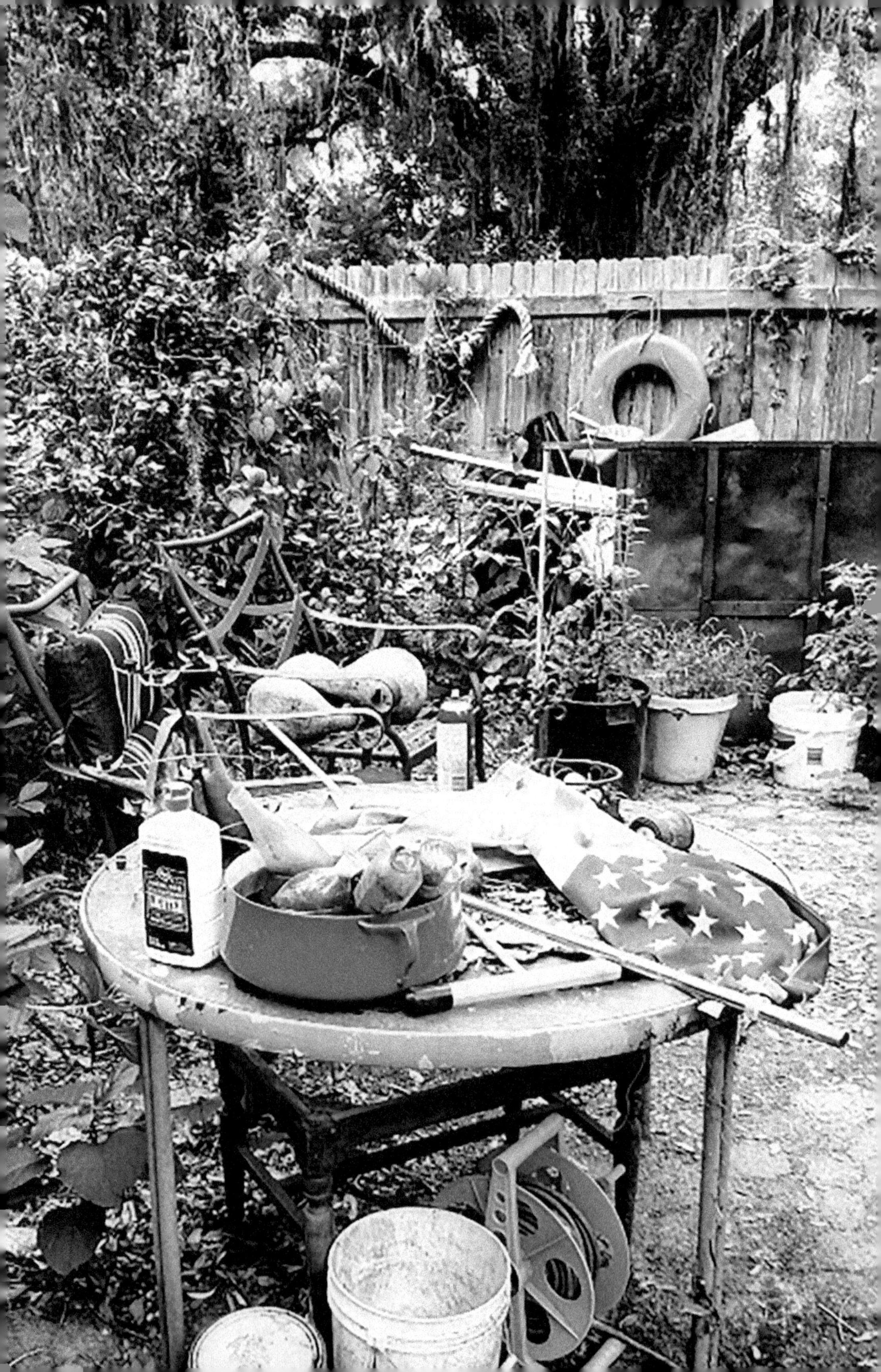

Factors

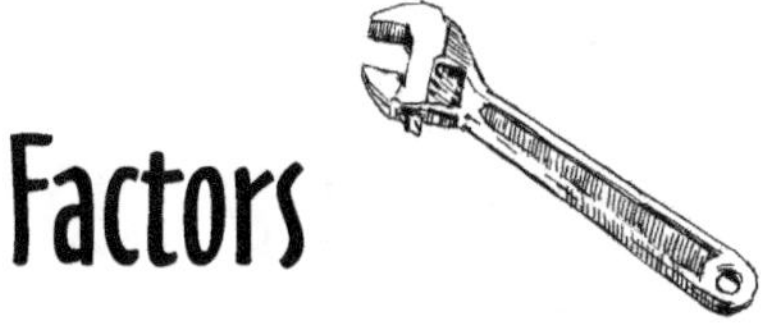

As I try to match
morning stillness
mood
phase
moon phase
a sky without color

lush
tropic
branches
fruit tree
spill over
fence line
yet to fully
ripen
like blade o' grass
has its own drape-a-dew

match the
morning quiet
tender thoughts … wistful feeling

imagine
two cups of coffee
not just one

yours table-top
next to mine

me
next to
you

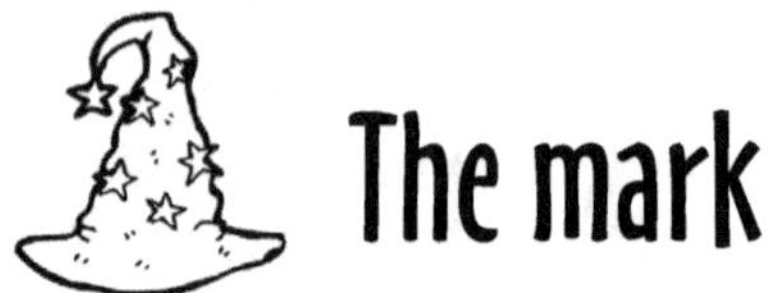

The mark

There is a mark you left on my breast
you were kissing me
passionate
lightning flashes shot through
as we danced on my back
behind the bar
I wanted you from the start
melting into your accented words
marveling at our common ground
you called me baby
the first time you called
compact combustibles
on chenille covered wood
I yielded wanting you inside

This morning I giggled
serving myself coffee from the urn
on the corner of the bar
ignoring resistance I peeked around and saw us there
the badge of your kiss
upon me

Madness afoot

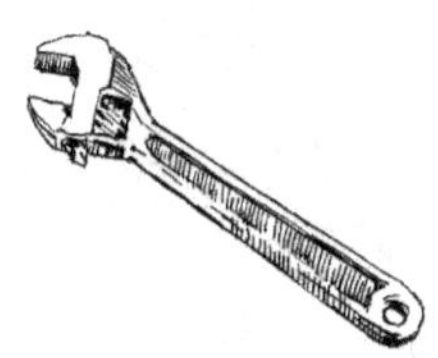

Coming up pass to
Nevada City
drunk on cough syrup
with empty red gas
fumes
still booking at seventy
call out names
of forgot gangsters
loaded .45 on passenger seat
feeling like some old
country song … "Dead Man's Curve"
pull into a Sunblock station
fuel up … corduroy pants … leather vest
fifty-six bucks and time is a'wastin'
roll on baby … make the night
sing tremble desperate for
salvation … redemption….relief
Panama red twist … sang 'bout that
back in '68 or so
Ghost town she-devil … calling fingernail pool hall
bingo numbers … outta some NBC mike … on a
silver platter sideways
skate into my own mad max dreamscape
not even pay toll exact change lane
yellow light flash … as thunder pass marks
exit only … on some side wind expressway
nightmare

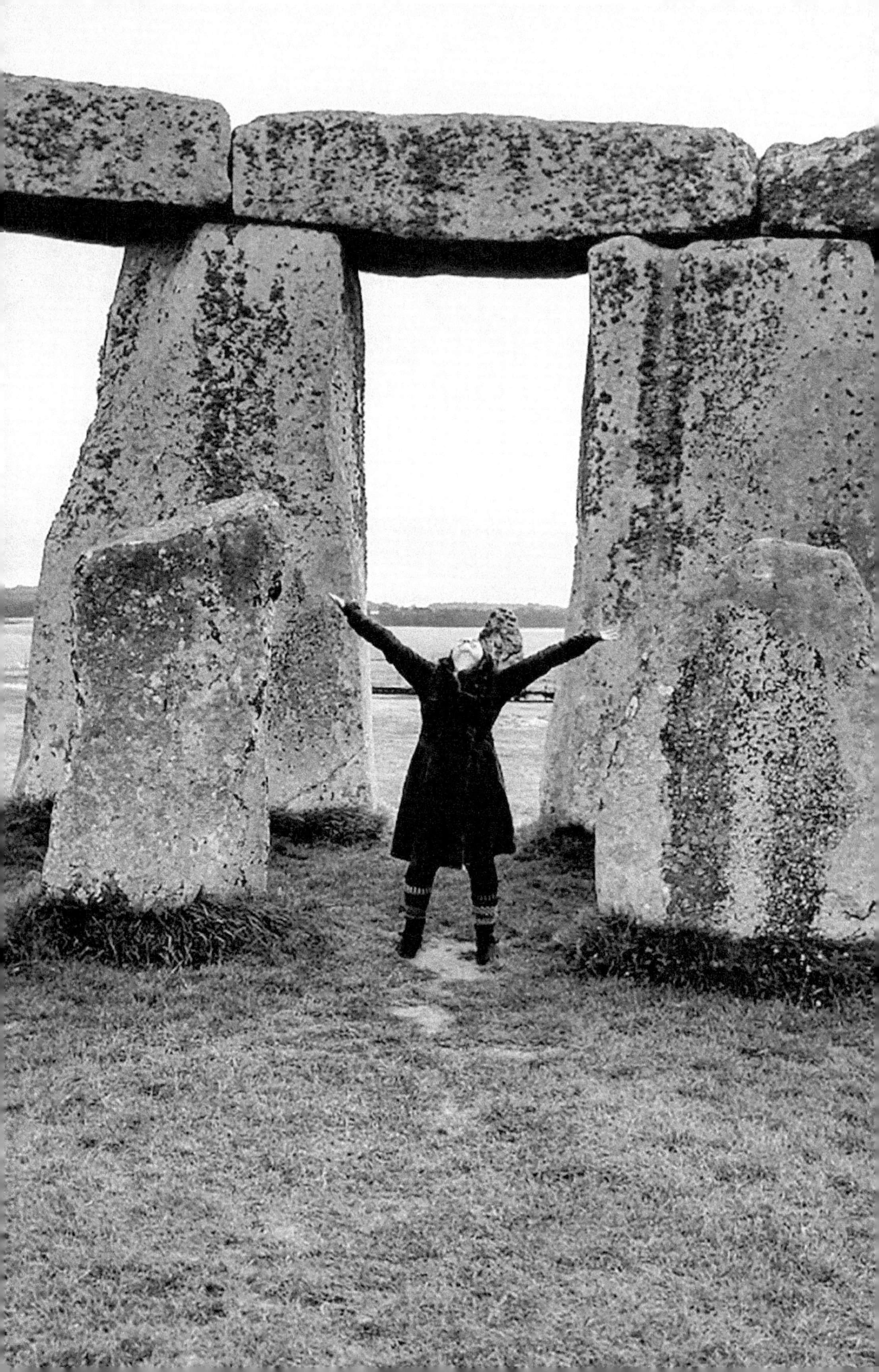

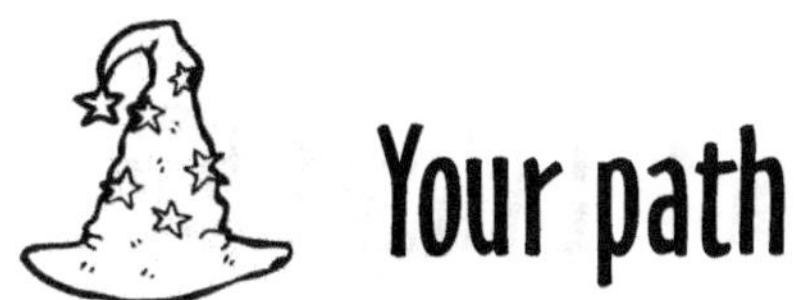

Your path

I can't figure it out for you
that's a path
you've got to take
on your own
make it easy
ask questions
listen
open
wider
while I sit
in a cave
I built from
your words
staring up
at Saturn
in the obsidian sky

Wacked-out, twisted logic

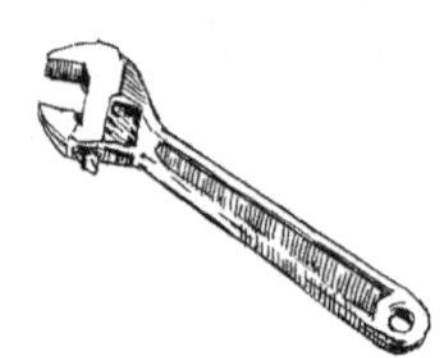

A woman alone
reading or
searching for
information
online or in public
is not
prey
yet
all these laptop
commandos
alive
in mom's basement
drinking
can after can
of Monster
both the liquid
plus mental variety
who fancy
themselves
some latter-day Romeo
of cyberspace
make rude or semi-obsessive
fools of themselves
reeling in their own
self-important
delusion
willy wackin'
perpetual adolescence

I got bad news for 'em
no man is a man
till a woman
teaches him
what a man is
vice versa
too
but less so
women know more
but have less reasons
to have to prove it
all the time

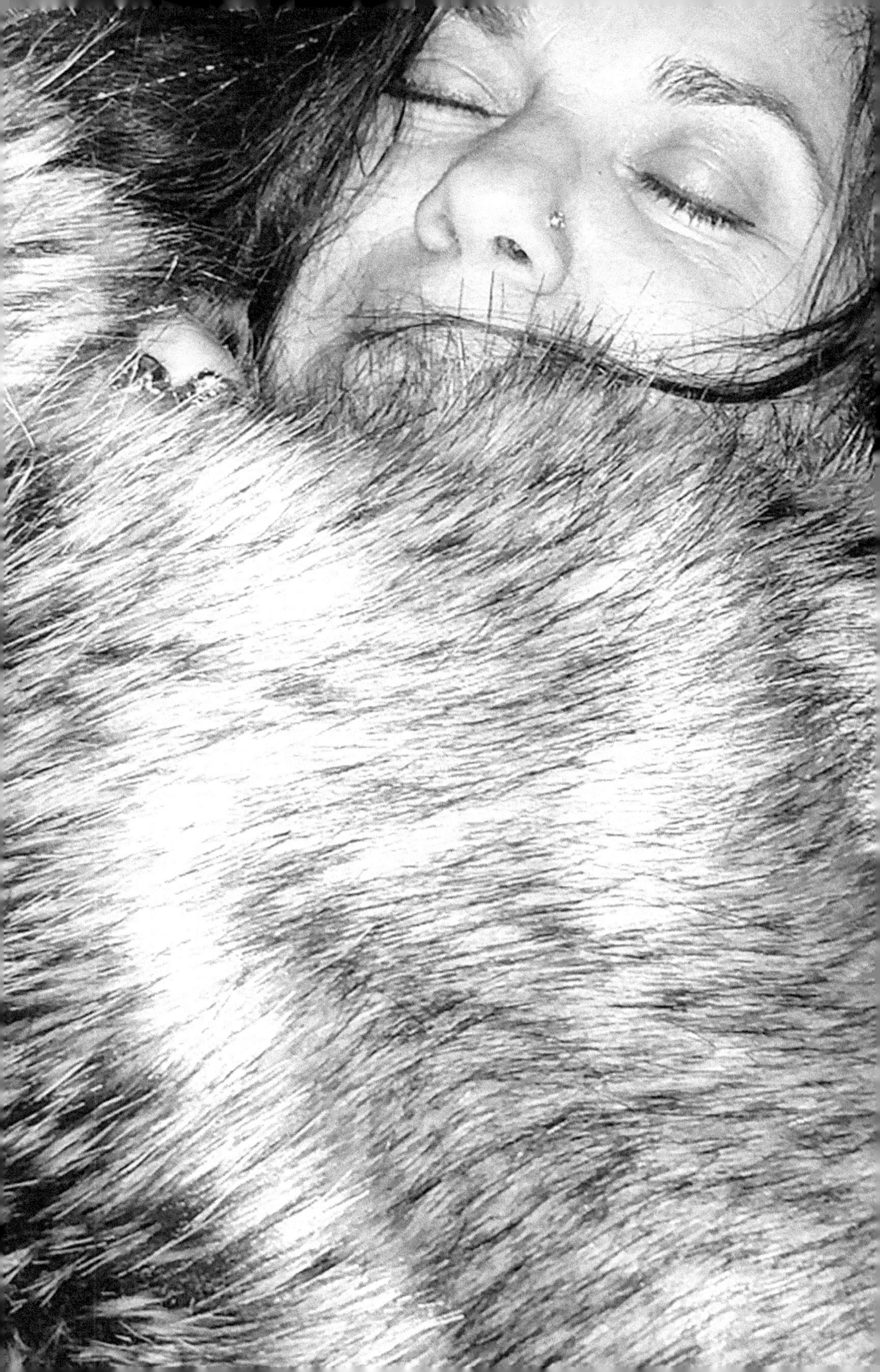

Uncaged

I climbed out of my cage
Lit some sage
Put on some Jimmy Page
And began the transformation

As I started to improve
I got into the groove
And was making my move
Toward the prophecy

That I would succumb
Keep my fight to minimum
Pull the parts to a sum
And surrender

Flying hot like a meteor
Bringing it to the exterior
I became the warrior
And fought the battle

Realizing what just occurred
That I had given my word
I flew free like a bird
To the next dimension

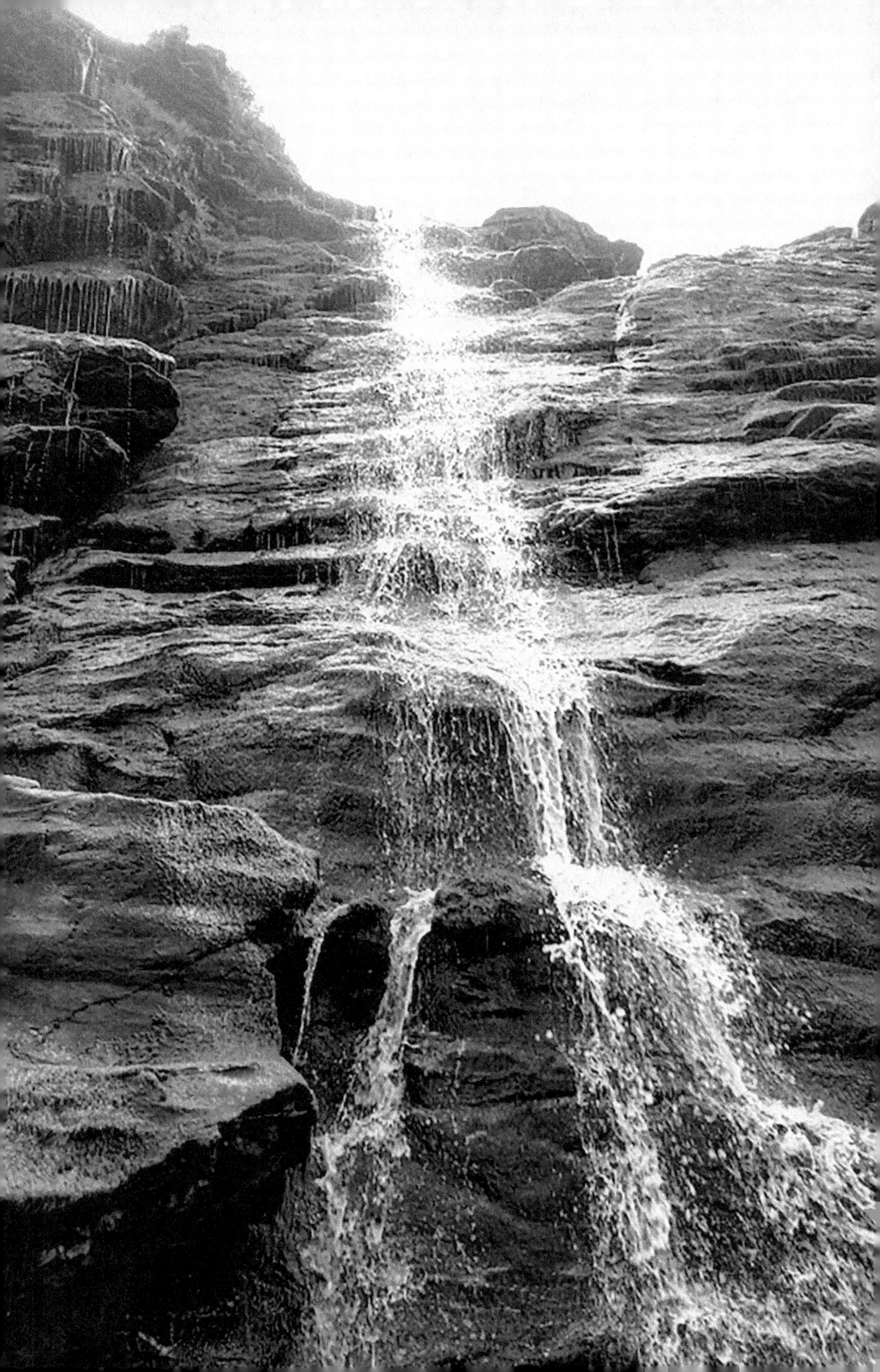

April 3, 2017

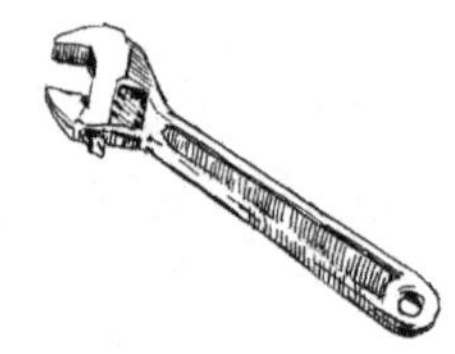

Are real paper and ink books just too heavy for ya?
does this addiction
to electronic fade fad wave band
connected just mean ya ...
o too cool to sit still and turn pages ...

O I always forget the mass hysteria of looking busy,
you know ...
that pop up that annoying beep
ya got a message,
from the amalgamated department of social hipness...

Tell ya ...
if ya don't app ...
this yr L7 for days ...

and sit here am I
turning pages,
escaping the weight of the world,
only to wonder

if my hero here is gonna get away
or have my hopes dashed
adventure in Norway
and I never left the house
the next big thing, is

ya take a pill

and the book flows
in ya blood stream
while ya scroll the phone
looking
for an answer
to questions
ya never even asked

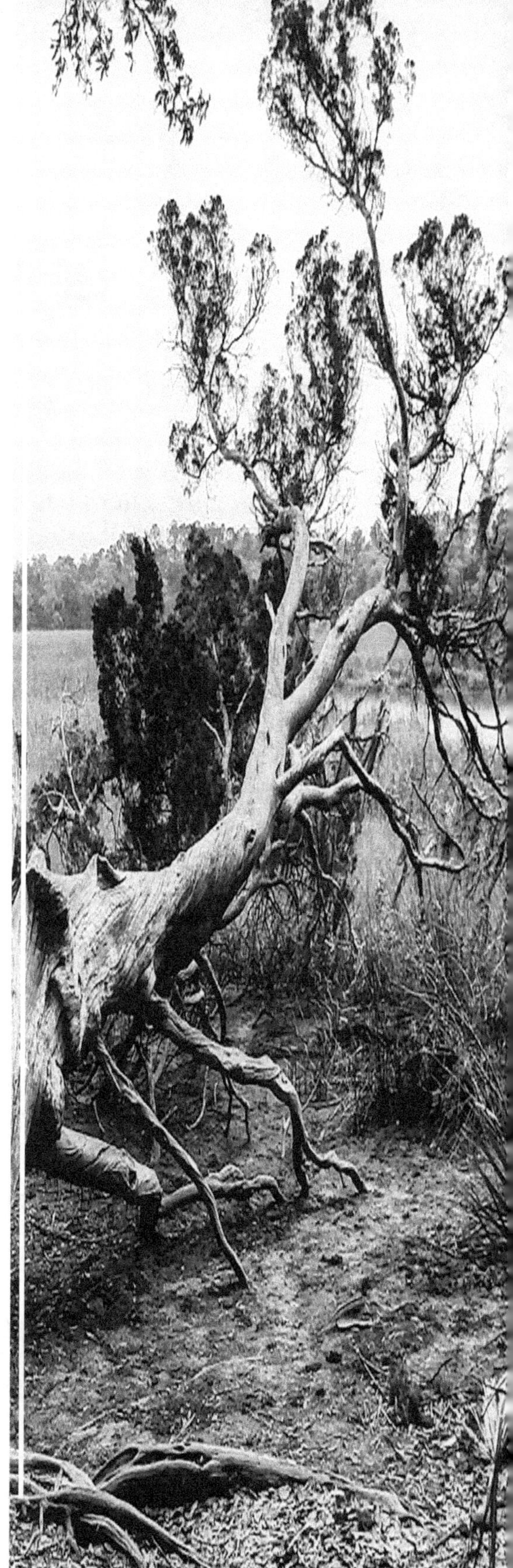

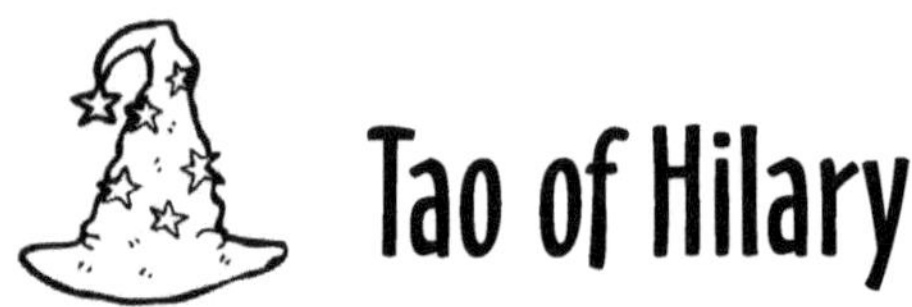

Tao of Hilary

The Tao according to Hilary, well what the hell's that?

You know the way it's supposed to be,
her dharma her philosophy
and whether you like it or not is of no concern you see
because I'm talking about Hilary.

To enter a room she must exhume whatever you've got hidden.
It makes her laugh when you're a gaffe
and she's touching what's forbidden.

An enormous sense of humor, a grooving baby boomer.

She's skipping down the Yellow Brick Road,
no time wasted kissing toads,
holding the deck, dealing abodes.
Whoa man it must be cool being Hilary.

Earth tones, precious stones, mortgage loans, flip phones,
delighted moans, danger zones.
Come on, you'll see what I mean.
Climb high upon Tibetan hills.
Amusement parks with screaming thrills.
Playing all the games of skill.
Nothing can compare. If you are weak beware.

To understand is not to know. To analyze is not to grow.
Don't judge it let it go and dig, the Tao, of Hilary.

Desiccated ball bounce-back

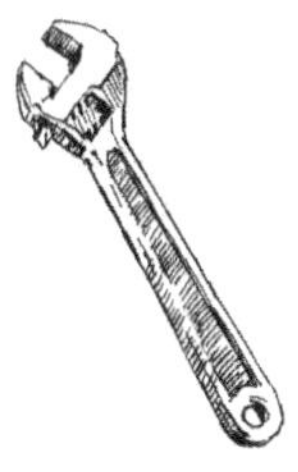

I
allowed
my
confusion over "love"
to
become a
drain on my resources
spending money
on kisses
that
I
never
got

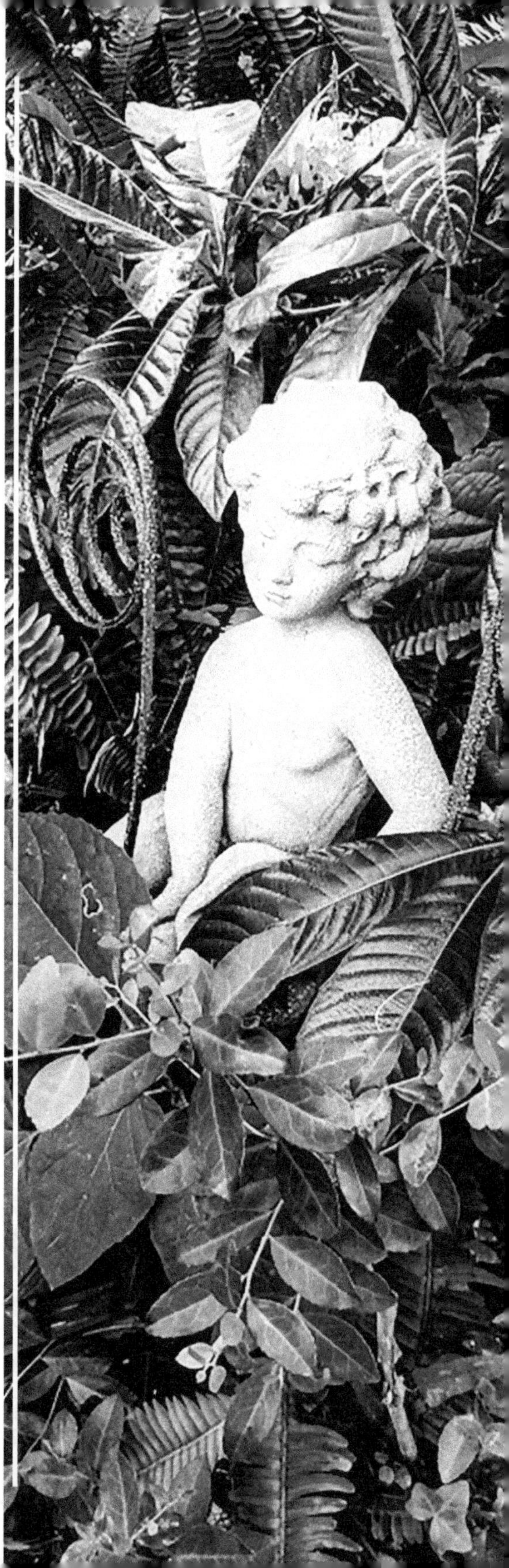

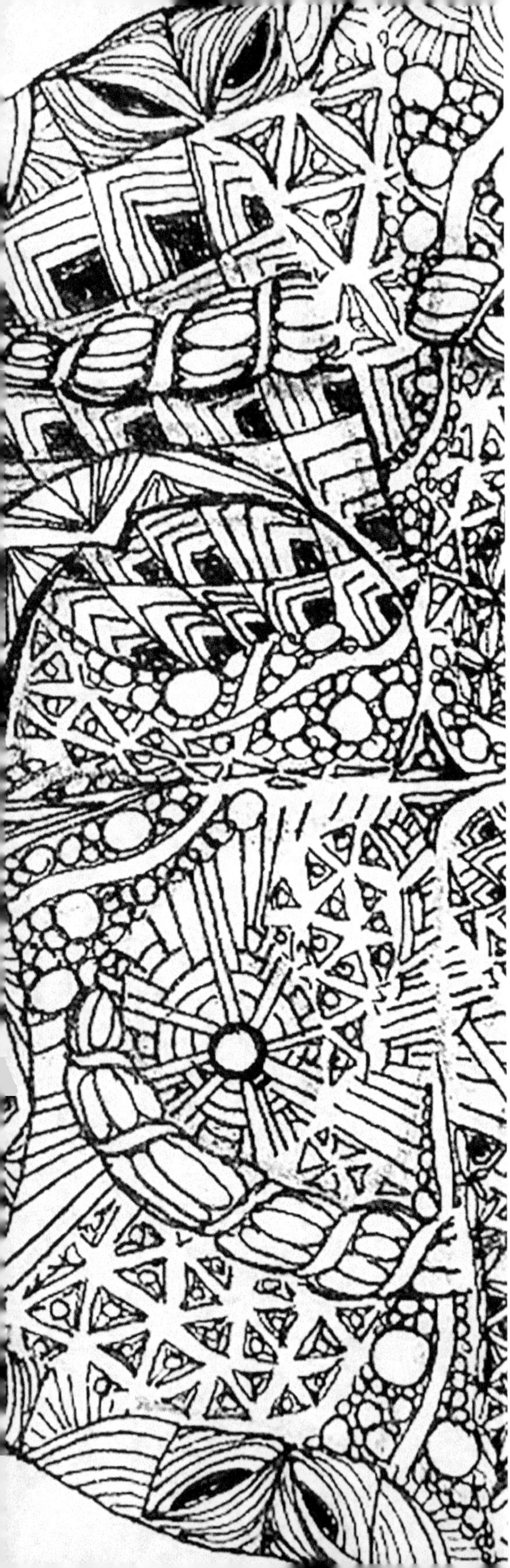

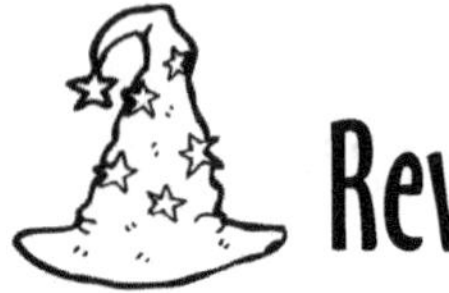

Revelation

We are fragments
tessellating star dust
cosmic poofs
of forgotten thoughts
chipping away
little by little

trying to leave
the good parts

it is shocking
how much
such a fragile
shard
can
take

All in, all in

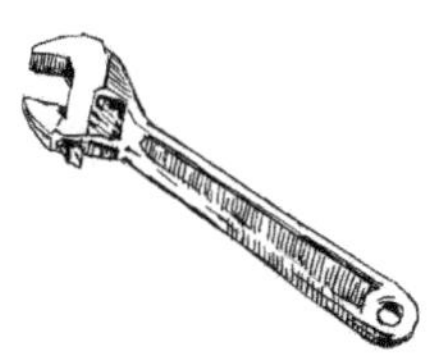

Those buried
have not voice

we here
must speak
of moral outrage

no arms, no legs
dented brains
suicide daily

uncounted vets in prison
homeless
dejected
rejected
support the troops boys
till ya get the stock bonus

as Decoration Day
pins a medal
on the grave
of one of my ol' comrades

I point out the hypocrisy
of those
who sit in an office
or in the A/C "war room"
plotting death tolls
against bottom line profit

rest you valiant brave souls
as cowards go to the symphony
to hear the *Flight of Valkyries* pat
'em self on the back
call 'em self-patriots

Cazzo a morte!

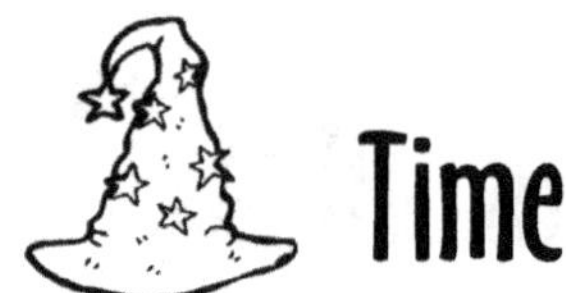

Time

Time moves marching
no regard
relentless
sweeping us
in a wave
drown
sink
swim
conform
accommodate

If there truly is free will
Do we have a choice?

Sit quietly
meditate
this is the
prime
directive
the needed buoyancy
to float with the
current

Was a time

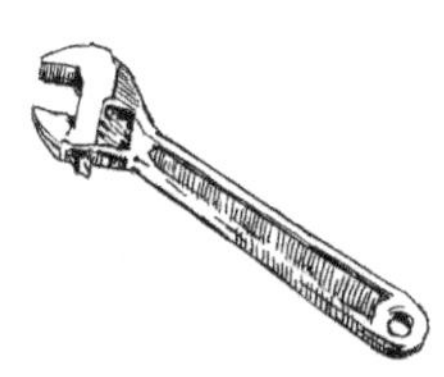

Was a time
I could make
motors sing
baritone
'n tires screech tenor
gears never slipped
U joints never broke
oil + water were good
now
well we
all
get
old

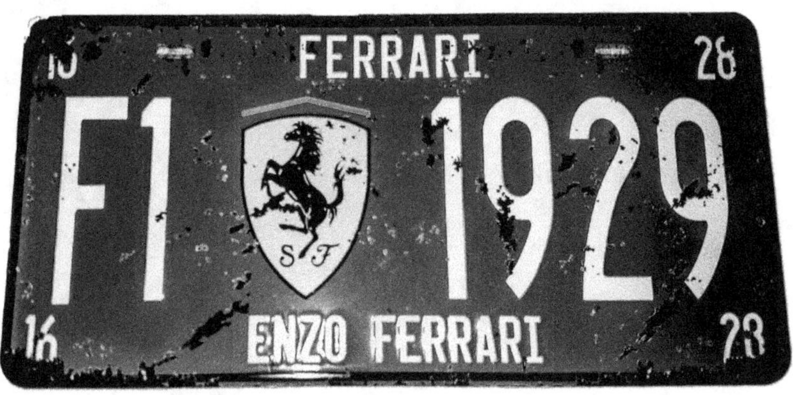

Your letters

I save your letters
like dried flower petals
and visit them
to breathe in
the essence
of our past conversations

your wisdom and candor
hang precariously upon
your take
on life
in this existence

I savor the moments
in between words

walking with you
and talking
or just sitting
in the mist once again

feeling the magic
as humming birds
do all the talking
with their wings

you are inside of me
I hear your laughter
and see your expressions

and even though apart
we are closer than ever

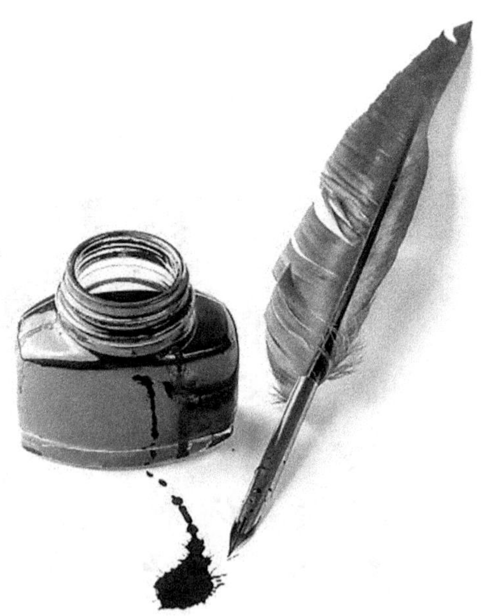

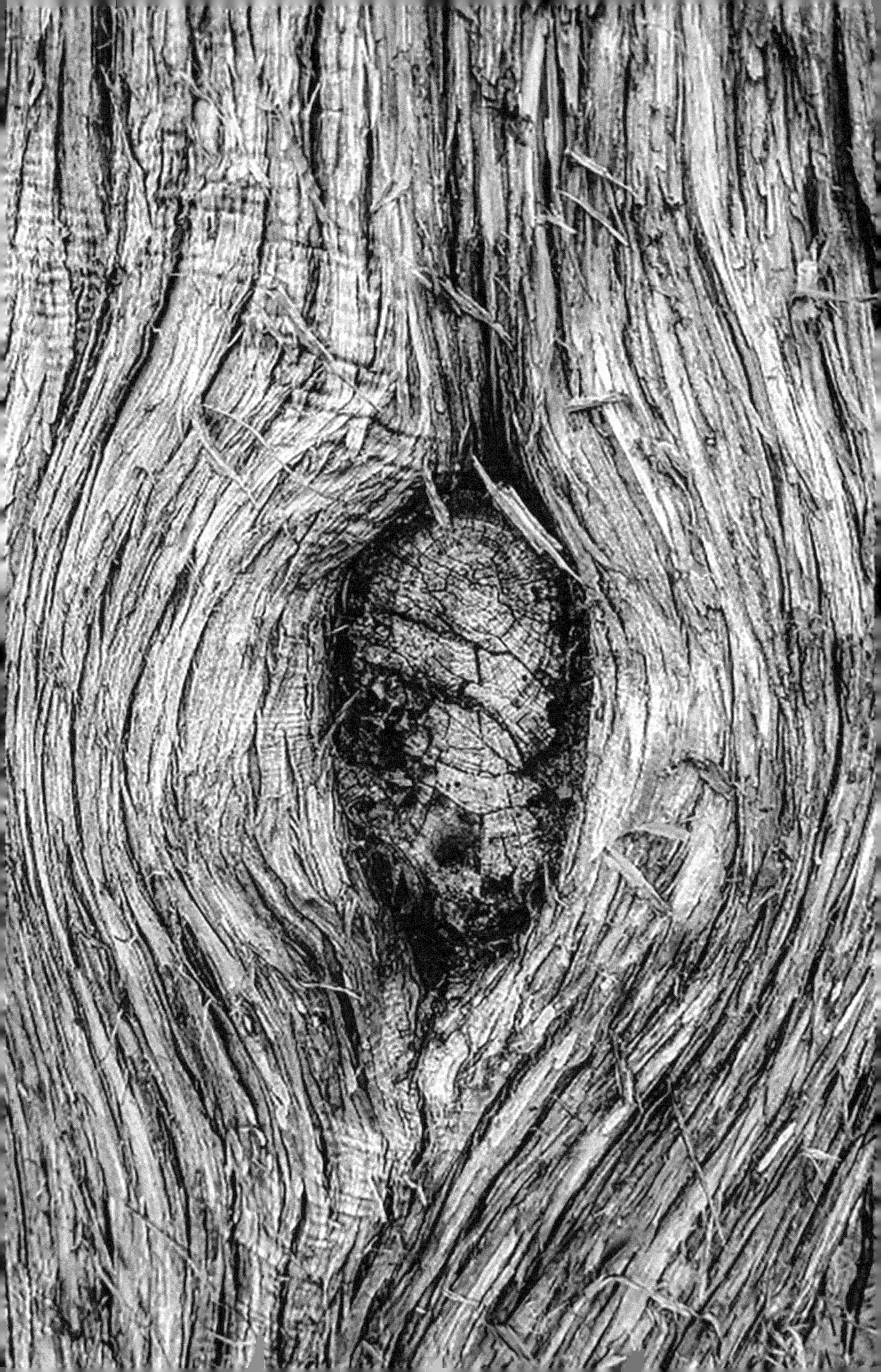

What people are saying about The Wizard and The Wrench

"The bold and brazen poetic genius of Dominic Albanese rattles in your head and cuts clear to the bone. Bukowski ain't got nothing on this former New Yorker. Ambika Devi summons the natural rhythms of our world to the surface so that we can peer down onto the still pond of human nature."

Ted Fauster
Speculative fiction author of The World of Faerel series and poet. www.tedfauster.com

"Some visionary doomed Italian Catholic lost Coney Island Americana liturgy of angels, stripped down V-8's, tarot readings—and goils."

Kris Saknussemm
Award-winning poet, short-story writer, novelist, and painter, head of the multimedia arts collective CLAMON. http://www.krissaknussemm.com/

"What are the chances that hardware and headwear would go hand in hand? Can you imagine the merging of magic and mechanics? Astrologer, yoga scholar/teacher, healer, and author Ambika Devi, with Vietnam War vet, mechanic, and biker-dude Dominic Albanese have joined forces to co-write The Wizard and the Wrench. This book of poetry provides a juxtaposition between the etheric and the earthy. An image of a wizard's hat and a wrench denotes the words of each. They volley back and forth, tempting the reader to laugh and shake their heads in knowing delight and sometimes amazement as the two share childhood memories about crayons and the aroma of a grandmother's cooking. Let your fancy be tickled by their words."

Edie Weinstein

MSW, LSW, is a colorfully creative journalist, inspiring speaker, licensed social worker, interfaith minister, editor, and author of The Bliss Mistress Guide To Transforming The Ordinary Into The Extraordinary. She calls herself an Opti-mystic who sees the world through the eyes of possibility.

www.opti-mystical.com

"Cutting the syllabic molecules through and through with a wizened clarity, with the air of twisting prose delicately and sublimely into metaphysically regulated, exquisite poetry. These two writers perpetuate positive, syncopated ear candy—simultaneously packed with language nutrition—*aixo era y no era* (it was and it was not)—and provide us with a singularly exotic pleasure. A word-fest fit for the finest gourmands of linguistic delicacies. I hope you enjoy these treasured sounds as both a feast for the soul, and as a massage for the ears, mind and chakras."

Dr. Patagonia

Poet

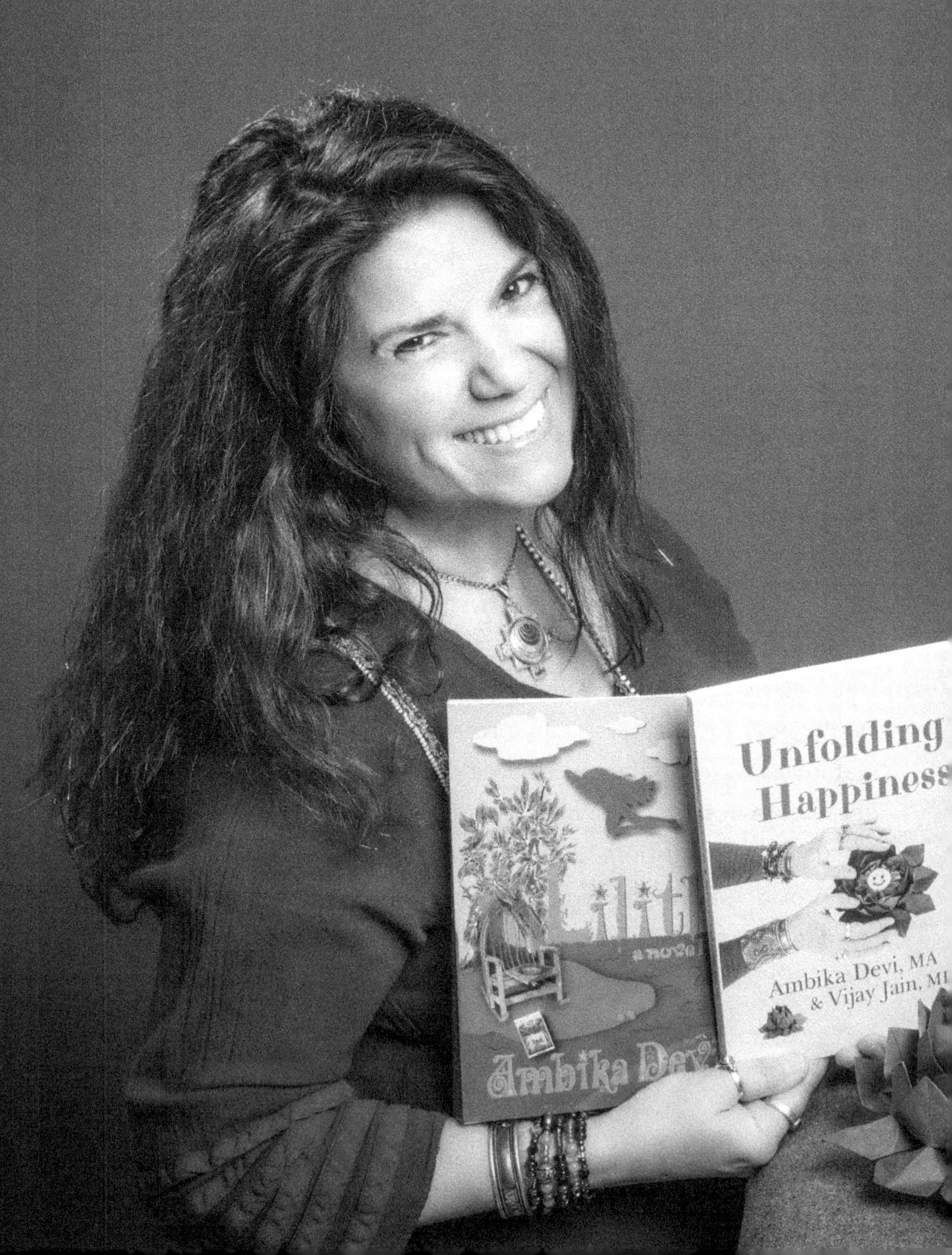
Unfolding
Happines
Ambika Devi, MA
& Vijay Jain, MI
Ambika Dev

About the Authors

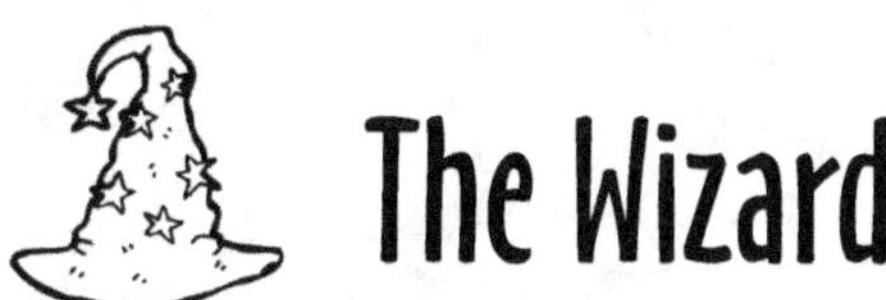

The Wizard

As a child, **Ambika Devi** filled the margins of her notebooks with original stories, drawings, and poetry. This mystified her teachers but, thankfully, that did not stop her.

She went on to write her first novel, *Lilith,* which was a finalist in the 2015 International Book Awards in the category of Spiritual Fiction. This was followed by her second book, *Unfolding Happiness,* a treatise of happiness, health, and Ayurveda which was named one of the Top Hundred Indie published books of 2016 under her newly hatched publishing house, Mythologem Press.

Ambika's backpack is stuffed with colored pens, a journal, a Kindle, a passport, and a deck of Tarot Cards. Her lifelong romance with the written word and belief that story time is the sweet medicine of existence keep her connected with academia. Currently Ambika is Dean of Psychic Arts and Professor of Divination, Healing, Psychic Arts, and Magickal Practices for the Grey School of Wizardry, and she is a mentor for the Yoga-Samskrutham University.

Ambika spends a lot of time floating in the celestial ocean. Her loving humor, mystical wisdom, and colorful cosmic insight fly off the pages of her books and into the hearts of her readers.

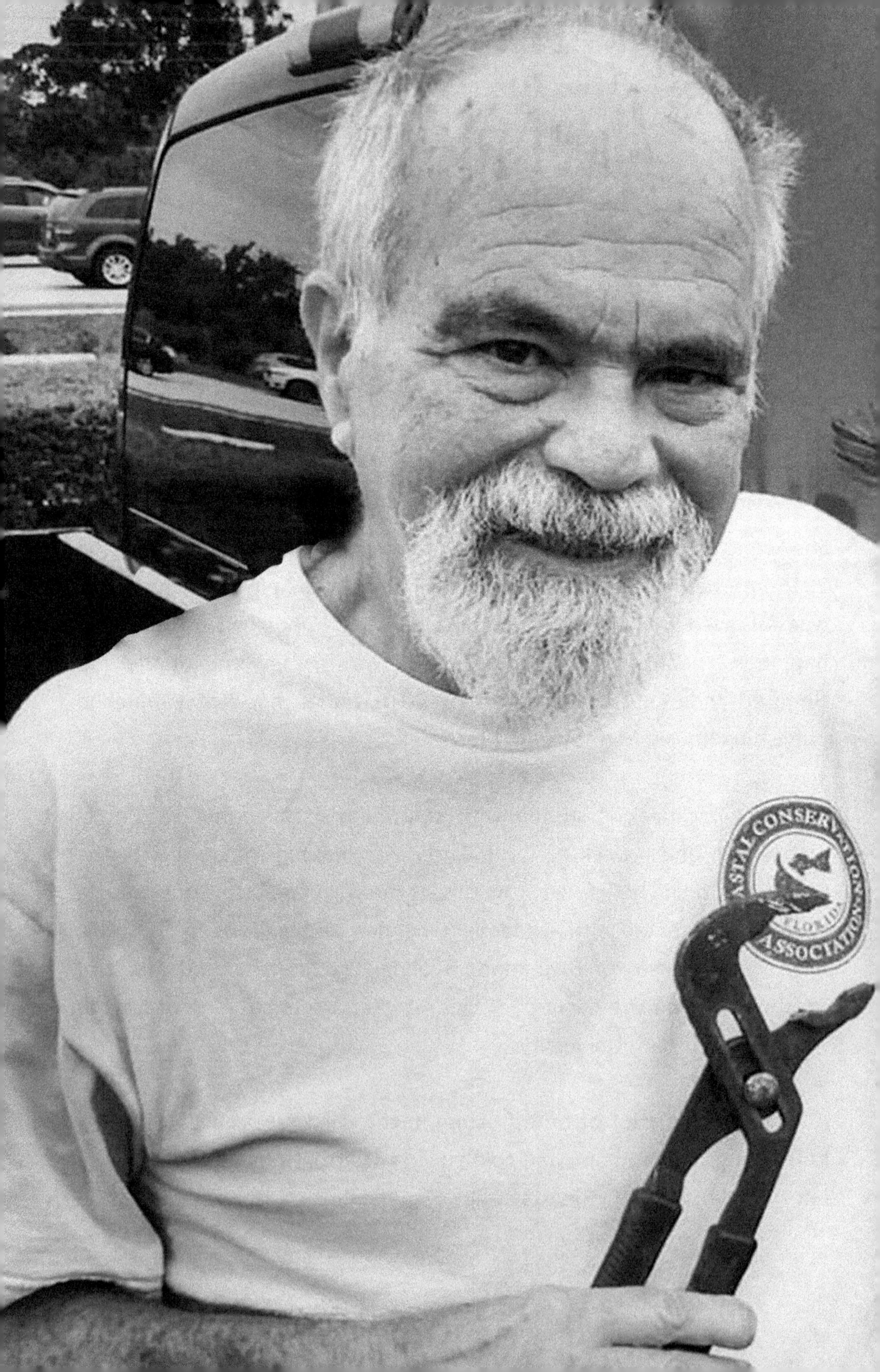
ASTAL CONSERVATION
FLORIDA
ASSOCIATION

The Wrench

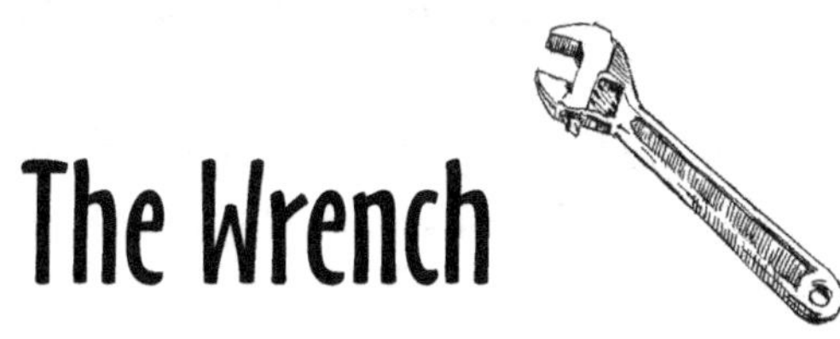

Dominic Albanese was born in Hell's Kitchen three months after the atomic bomb dropped. His half-Italian, half-Irish roots have been a source of confusion, bemusement, and amusement, sustaining him through his family's move to Coney Island at age six and, later, when he dropped out of school in the seventh grade to work in a gas station on Neptune Avenue. There he got involved with some chop shop guys and was caught. The family's priest and his dad, along with the cop who popped him, forged his birth records to make him two years older. Five minutes later, he was enlisted in the army.

He went to work for Nick Torelli in 1967, on cars that belonged to all the San Francisco rock stars, dope-dealers, lawyers, doctors, and assorted wannabes. Later he was sent to Italy for training twice by Ferrari, and once to England by Jaguar. Dominic twisted wrenches on some of the best cars in the world for more than forty years. In 2009 he retired to swim, walk, go fishing, and write poetry. Now a septuagenarian, having turned seventy-two in November 2017, he says that for the first time in his life, he feels he has very few worries other than a yearly depression that creeps into his writing between Christmas and Easter, which proves his native roots are strong. Once he gets a handle on it, he remembers that he lives close to the ocean, where he can fish and kayak and get back to acting like he's twenty-two again.

More titles from Dominic: *Note Book Poems, Iconic Whispers, Bastards Had the Whole Hill Mined, Then and Now, Love is Not Just a Word,* and *Only the River Knows.*

Photographs and original artwork credits

- Orchard, Michael. 2018. Digital photograph. Reprinted with permission. (pp. 4-5)
- Bezembinder Wyant, Cristine. 2013. Digital Photograph. Reprinted with permission. (p. 6)
- Rueda Duque, Catalina. 2018. Digital photograph. Reprinted with permission. (p. 7)
- Rueda Duque, Catalina. 2018. Black and white digital photograph. Reprinted with permission. (p. 8)
- Rueda Duque, Catalina. 2018. Black and white digital photograph. Reprinted with permission. (p. 9)
- Rueda Duque, Catalina. 2018. Digital photograph. Reprinted with permission. (p. 10)
- Ambika Devi. 2018. Black and white digital photograph. Reprinted with permission. (p. 13)
- Rueda Duque, Catalina. 2018. Digital photograph. Reprinted with permission. (p. 15)
- Rueda Duque, Catalina. 2018. Black and white digital photograph. Reprinted with permission. (p. 16)
- Rueda Duque, Catalina. 2018. Digital photograph. Reprinted with permission. (p. 18)
- Devi, Ambika. 2018. Black and white digital photograph. Reprinted with permission. (p. 21)
- Ambika Devi. 2018. Digital photograph. Reprinted with permission. (pp. 22-23)
- Orchard, Michael. 2018. Digital photograph. Reprinted with permission. (p. 24)
- Devi, Ambika. 2018. Black and white digital photograph. Reprinted with permission. (p. 27)
- Devi, Ambika. 2018. Black and white digital photograph. Reprinted with permission. (p. 28)
- Devi, Ambika. 2018. Black and white digital photograph. Reprinted with permission. (p. 29)
- Rodriguez, Spain (1940-2012). 1977. Black ink illustration. (p. 31)
- Lee, Rusti. 2018. Black and white Digital photograph. Reprinted with permission. (pp. 32-33)
- Devi, Ambika. Black pen illustration. Reprinted with permission. (p. 34)
- Rueda Duque, Catalina. 2018. Black and white photograph. Reprinted with permission. (p. 37)
- Devi, Ambika. Digital photograph. Reprinted with permission. (p. 38)
- Rueda Duque, Catalina. 2018. Black and white photograph. Reprinted with permission. (p. 41)
- Devi, Ambika. 2018. Black and white digital photograph. Reprinted with permission. (p. 42)
- Rueda Duque, Catalina. 2018. Black and white photograph. Reprinted with permission. (p. 43)
- Devi, Ambika.2018. Digital photograph. Reprinted with permission. (p. 45)

- Devi, Ambika.2018. Digital photograph. Reprinted with permission. (pp. 46-47)
- Devi, Ambika.2018. Digital photograph. Reprinted with permission. (p. 48)
- Devi, Ambika. 2018. Black and white digital photograph. Reprinted with permission. (p. 51)
- Devi, Ambika. 2018. Black and white digital photograph. Reprinted with permission. (p. 53)
- Devi, Ambika. 2018. Digital photograph. Reprinted with permission. (p. 56)
- Bezembinder Wyant, Cristine. 2018. Digital Photograph. Reprinted with permission. (pp. 58-59)
- Rueda Duque, Catalina. 2018. Black and white photograph. Reprinted with permission. (p. 62)
- Rodriguez, Spain (1940-2012). 1969. Black ink illustration (p. 63)
- Rueda Duque, Catalina. 2018. Black and white photograph. Reprinted with permission. (p. 64)
- Devi, Ambika. Digital photograph. Reprinted with permission. (p. 65)
- Devi, Ambika. 2018. Digital photograph. Reprinted with permission. (p. 66)
- Devi, Ambika. 2018. Digital photograph. Reprinted with permission. (p. 69)
- Devi, Ambika. 2018. Digital photograph. Reprinted with permission. (pp. 72-73)
- Devi, Ambika. 2018. Black and white digital photograph. Reprinted with permission. (p. 74)
- Moon, Summer. 2018. Black and white digital photograph. Reprinted with permission. (p. 78)
- Devi, Ambika. 2018. Black and white digital photograph. Reprinted with permission. (p. 81)
- Devi, Ambika. 2018. Black and white digital photograph. Reprinted with permission. (p. 83)
- Devi, Ambika. 2018. Black and white digital photograph. Reprinted with permission. (p. 85)
- Devi, Ambika. 2018. Black and white digital photograph. Reprinted with permission. (p. 87)
- Devi, Ambika. 2018. Black ink illustration. Reprinted with permission. (p. 88)
- Devi, Ambika. 2018. Black and white digital photograph. Reprinted with permission. (p. 91)
- Rueda Duque, Catalina. 2018. Black and white photograph. Reprinted with permission. (p. 92)
- Devi, Ambika. 2018. Black and white digital photograph. Reprinted with permission. (p. 93)
- Devi, Ambika. 2018. Black and white digital photograph. Reprinted with permission. (pp. 94-95)
- Sturgess, Matt. 2017. Digital photograph. Reprinted with permission. (p. 96)
- Peckham, Gary. 2017. Digital photograph. Reprinted with permission. (p. 98)
- Devi, Ambika. 2018. Digital photograph. Reprinted with permission. (p. 102)

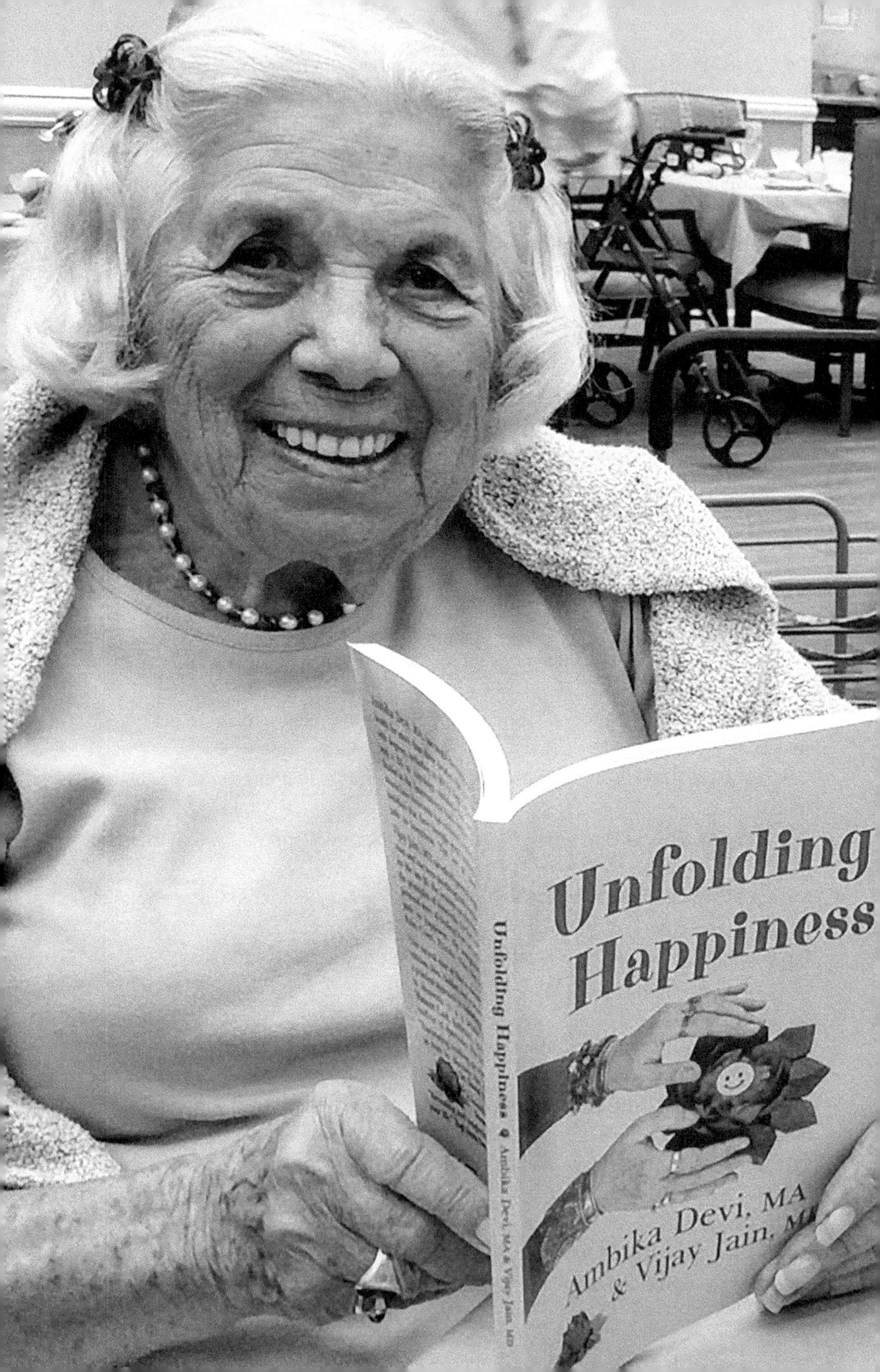
Unfolding
Happiness
Ambika Devi, MA
& Vijay Jain,
Unfolding Happiness

www.ingramcontent.com/pod-product-compliance
Lightning Source LLC
LaVergne TN
LVHW010935110826
845149LV00013B/2619
9780997867824